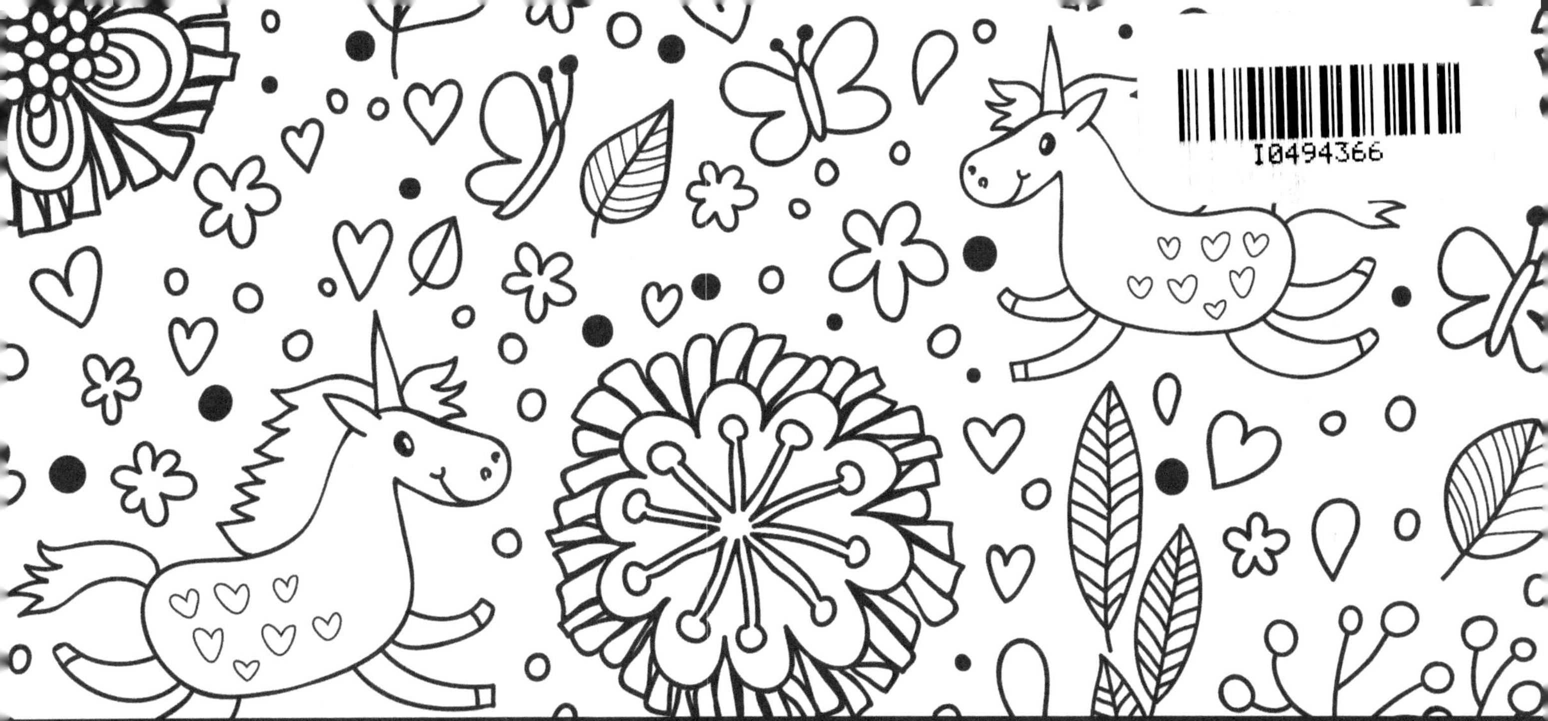

HEART
COLORING BOOK
FOR KIDS

▲ ART THERAPY COLORING

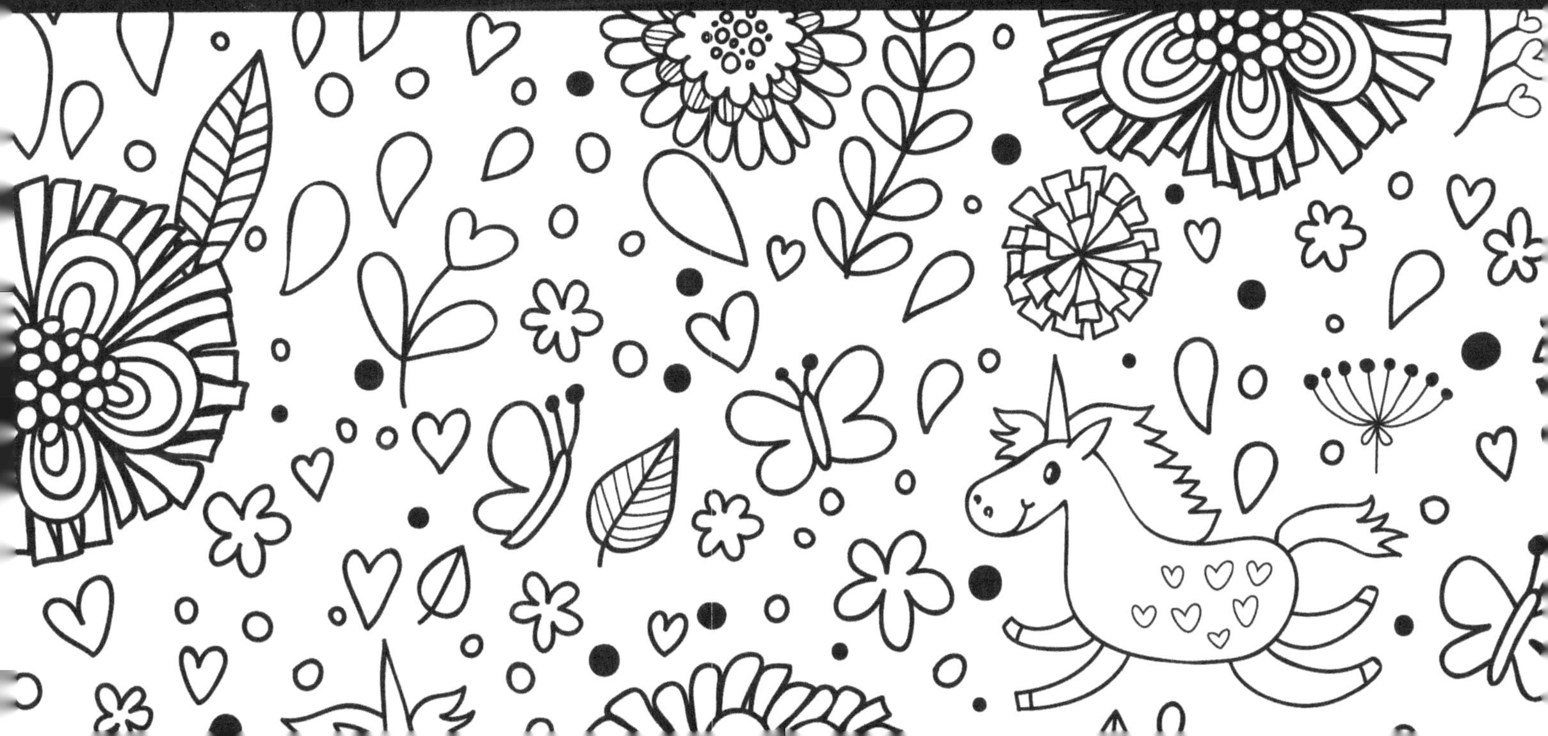

Preview of Coloring Pages

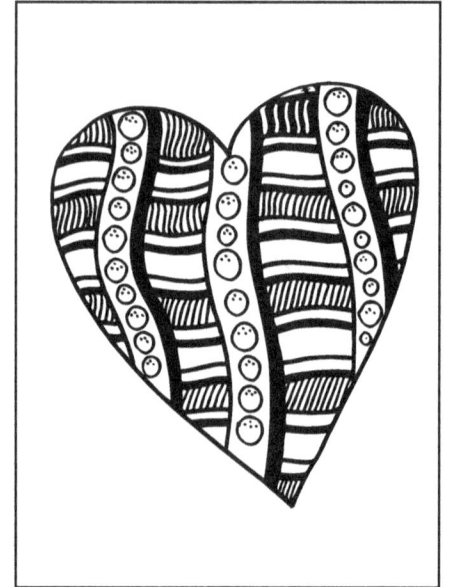
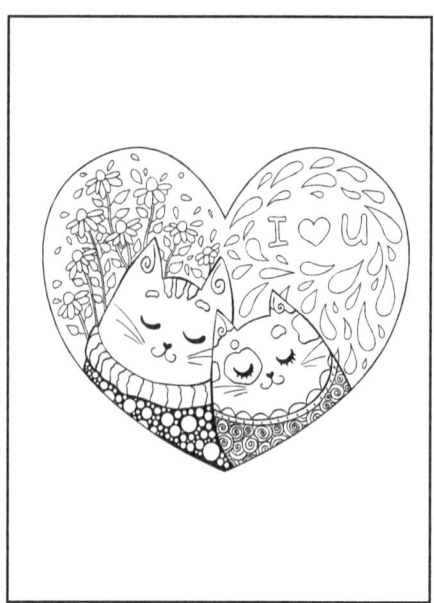
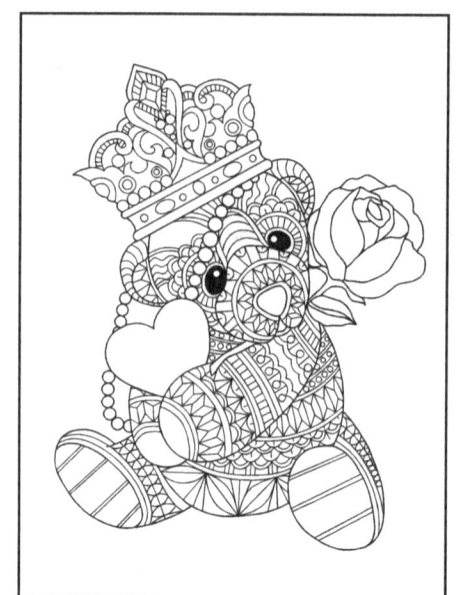
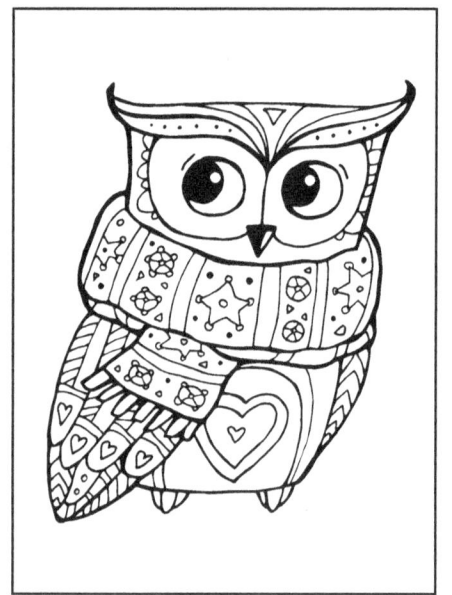
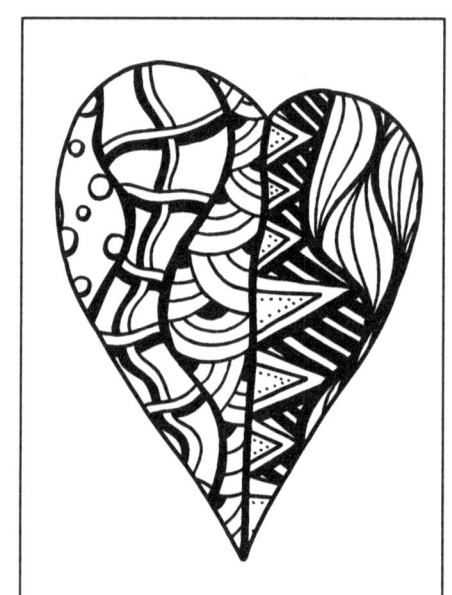
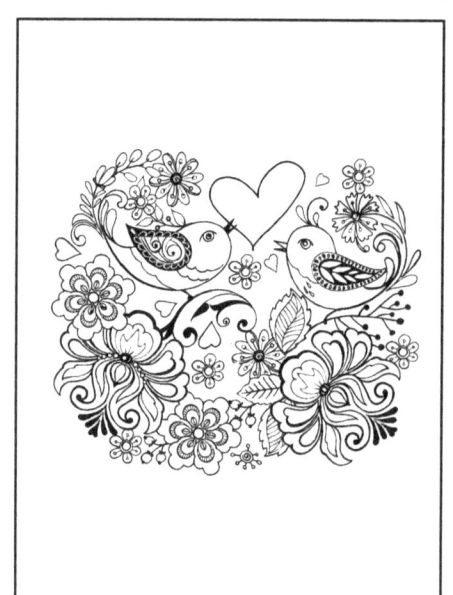
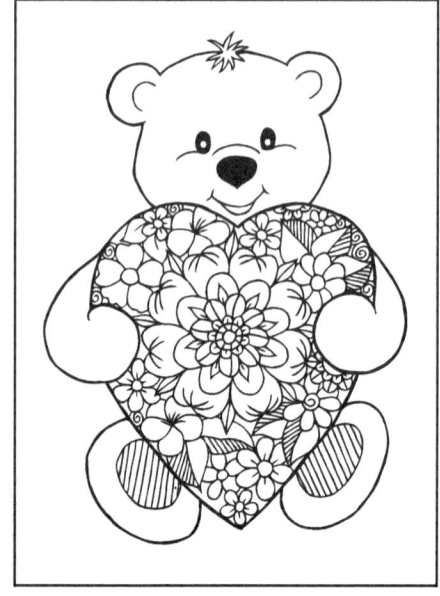
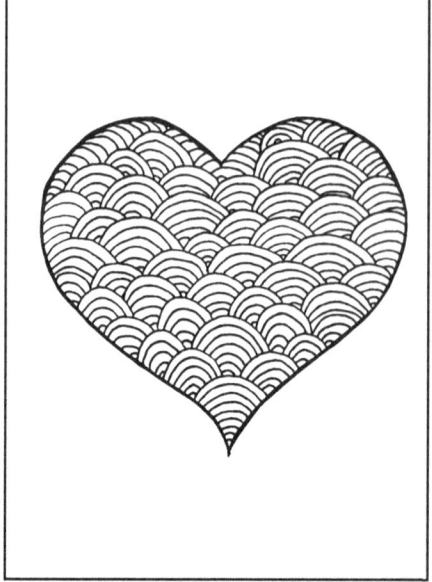
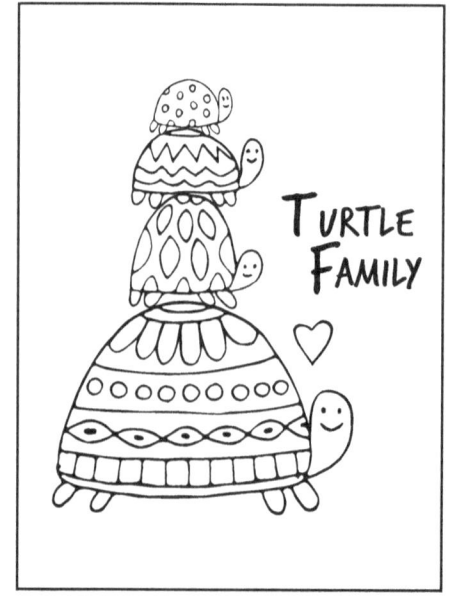

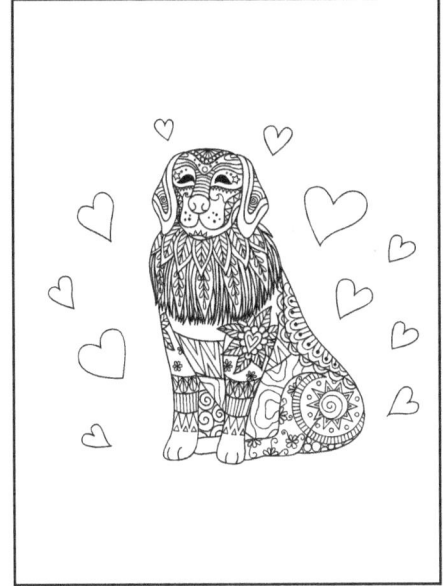
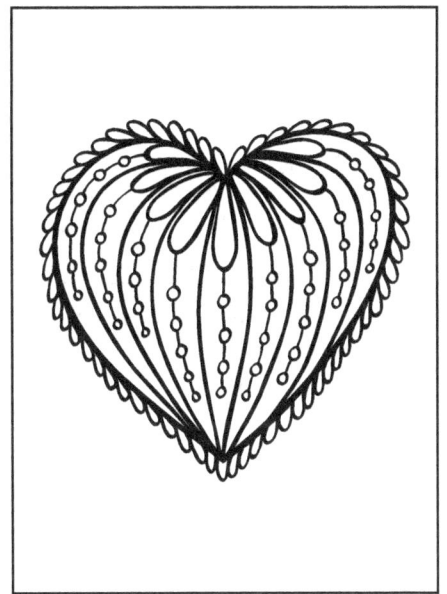
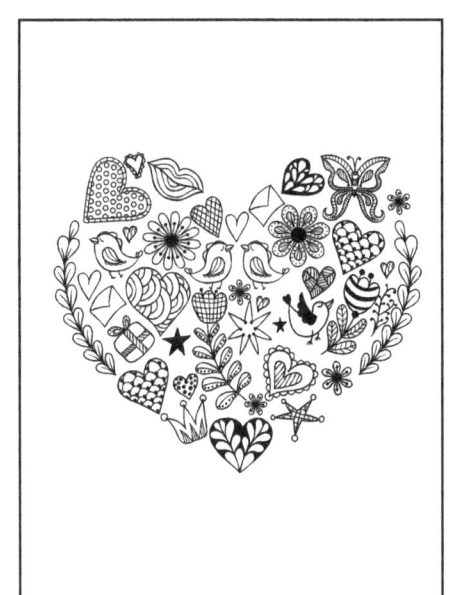
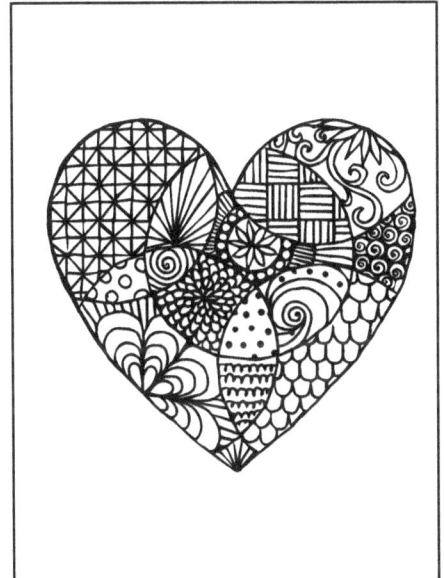
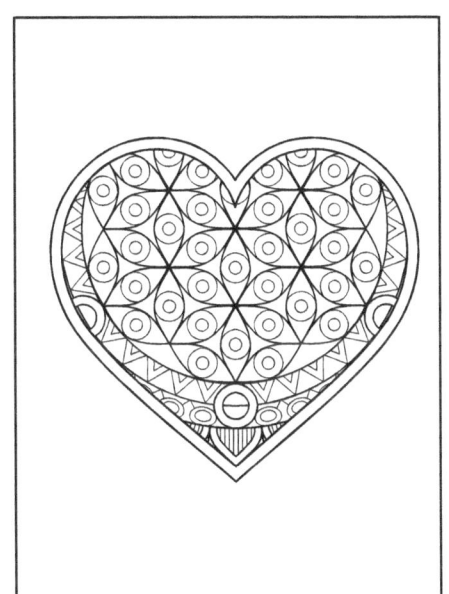
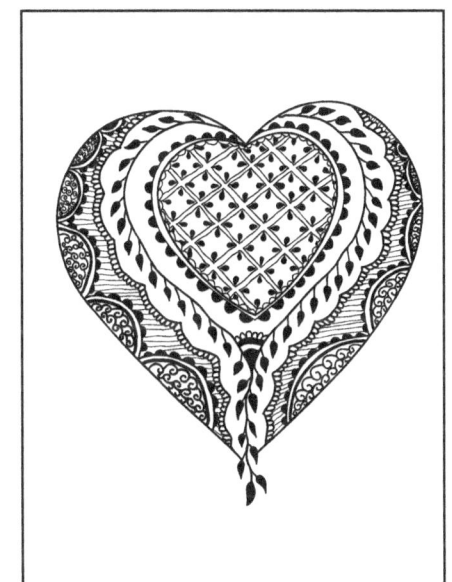
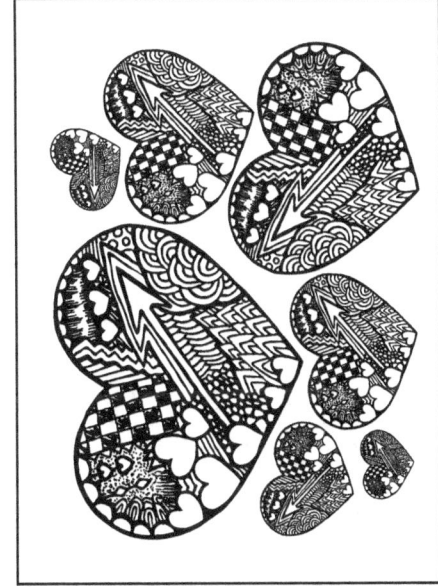
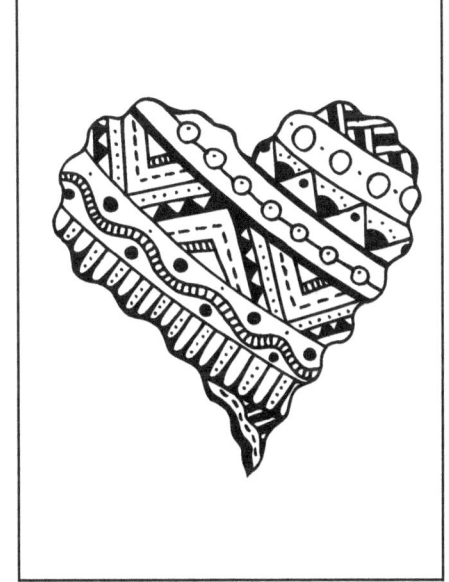
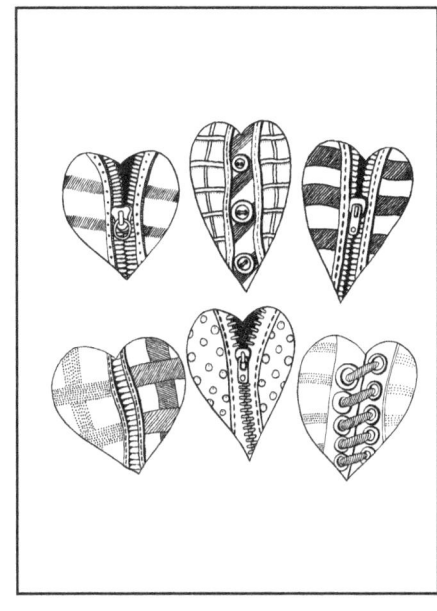

Preview of Coloring Pages

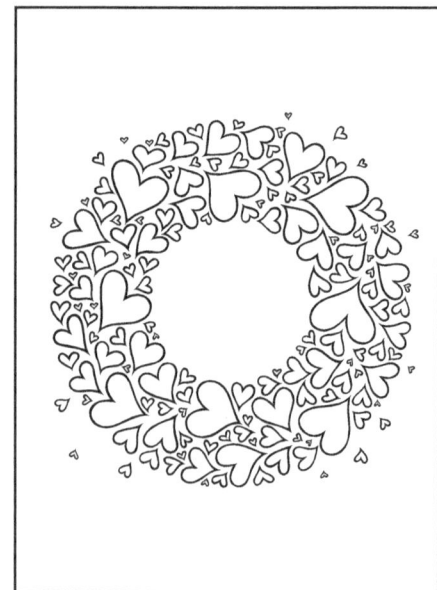 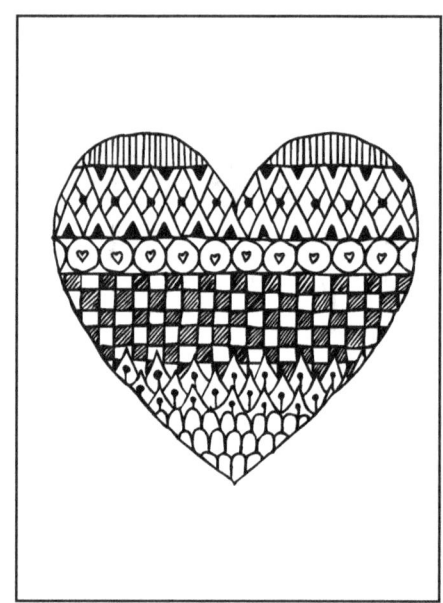 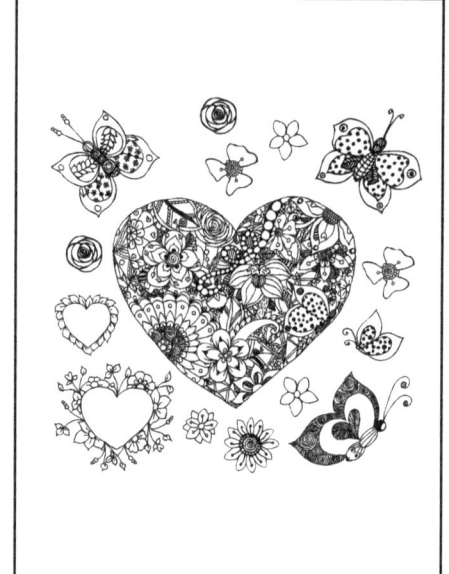

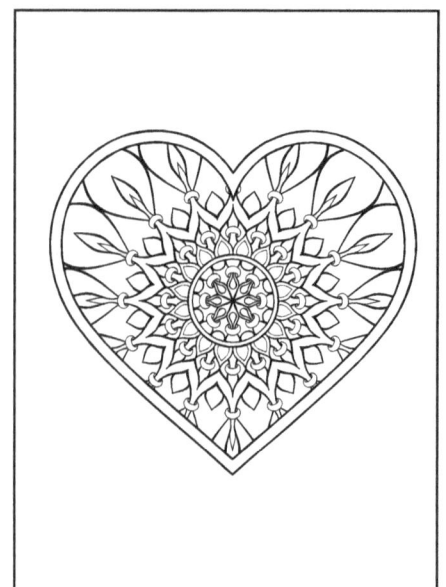 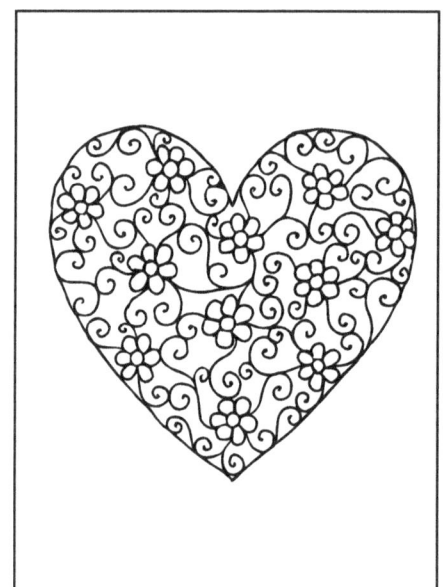 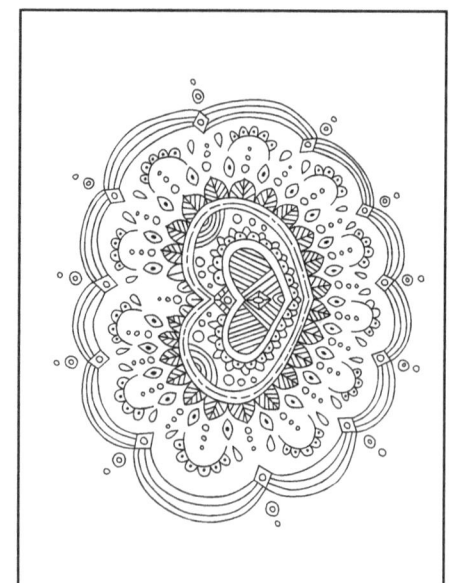

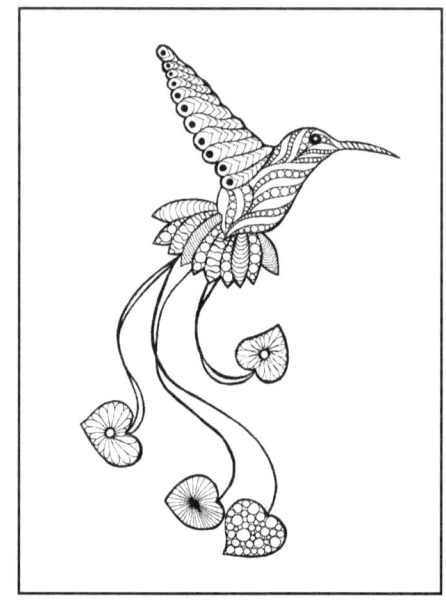 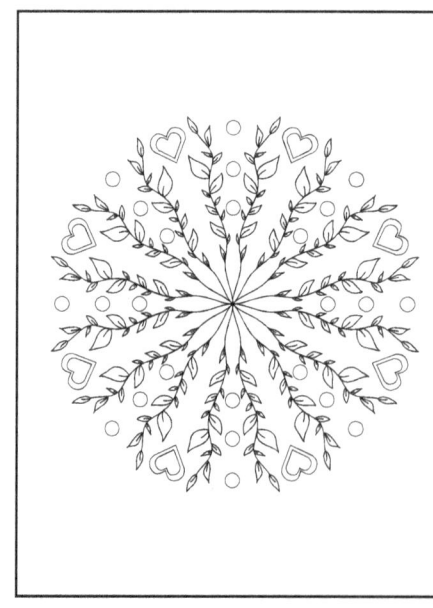 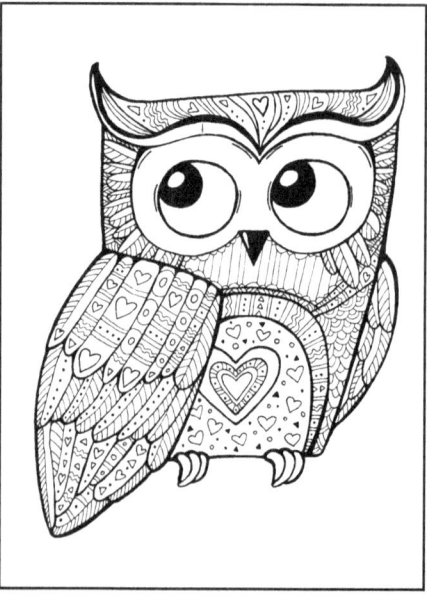

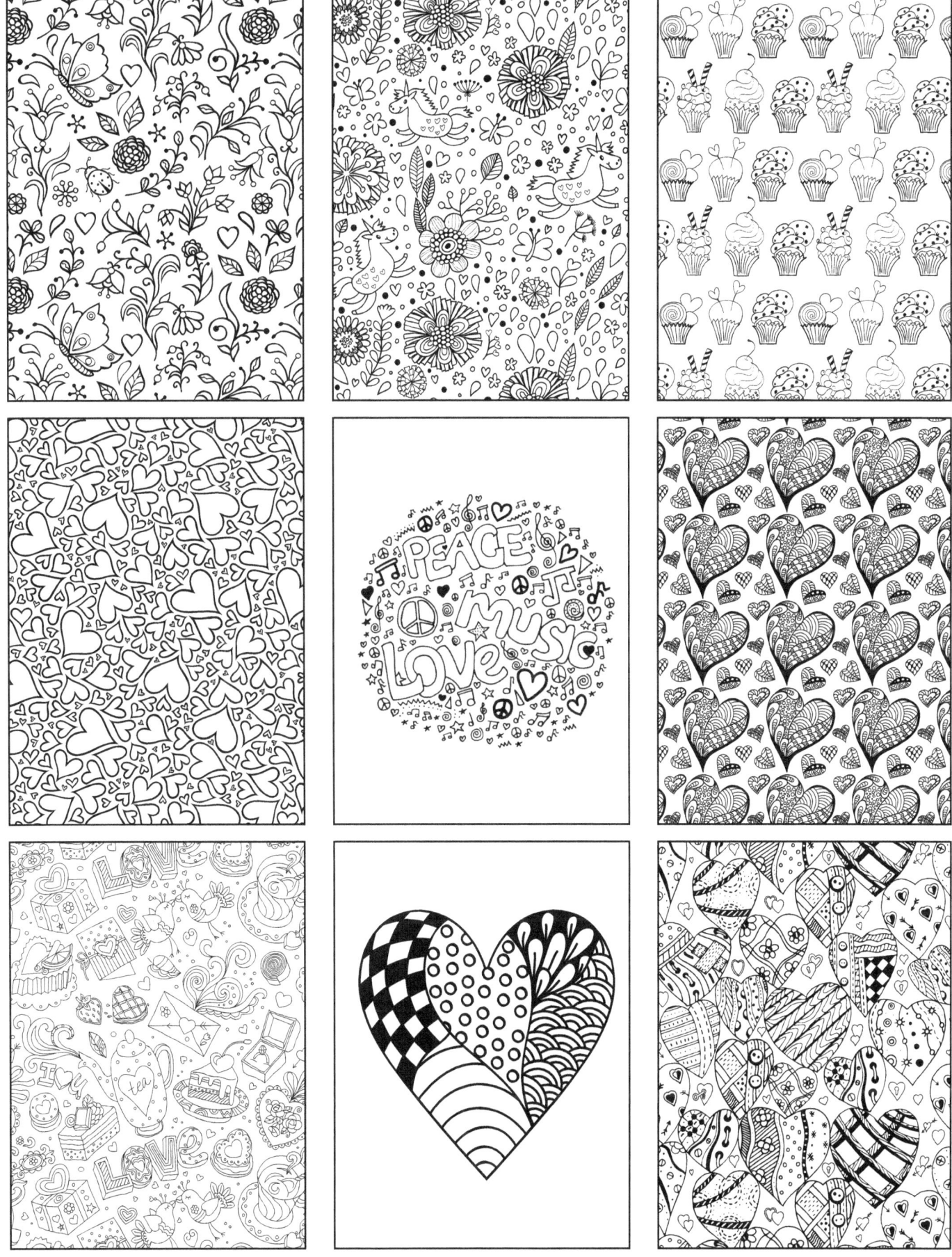

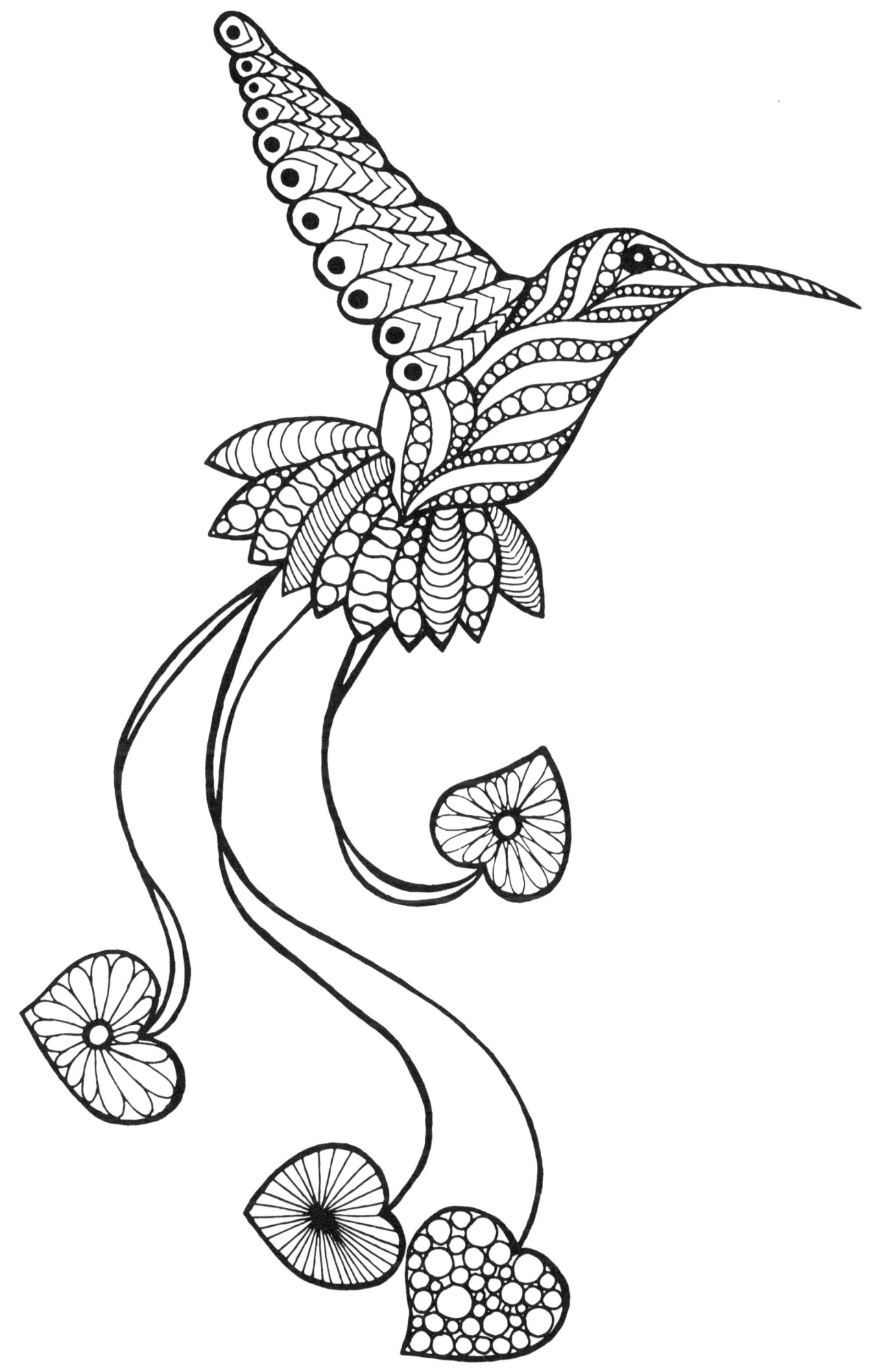

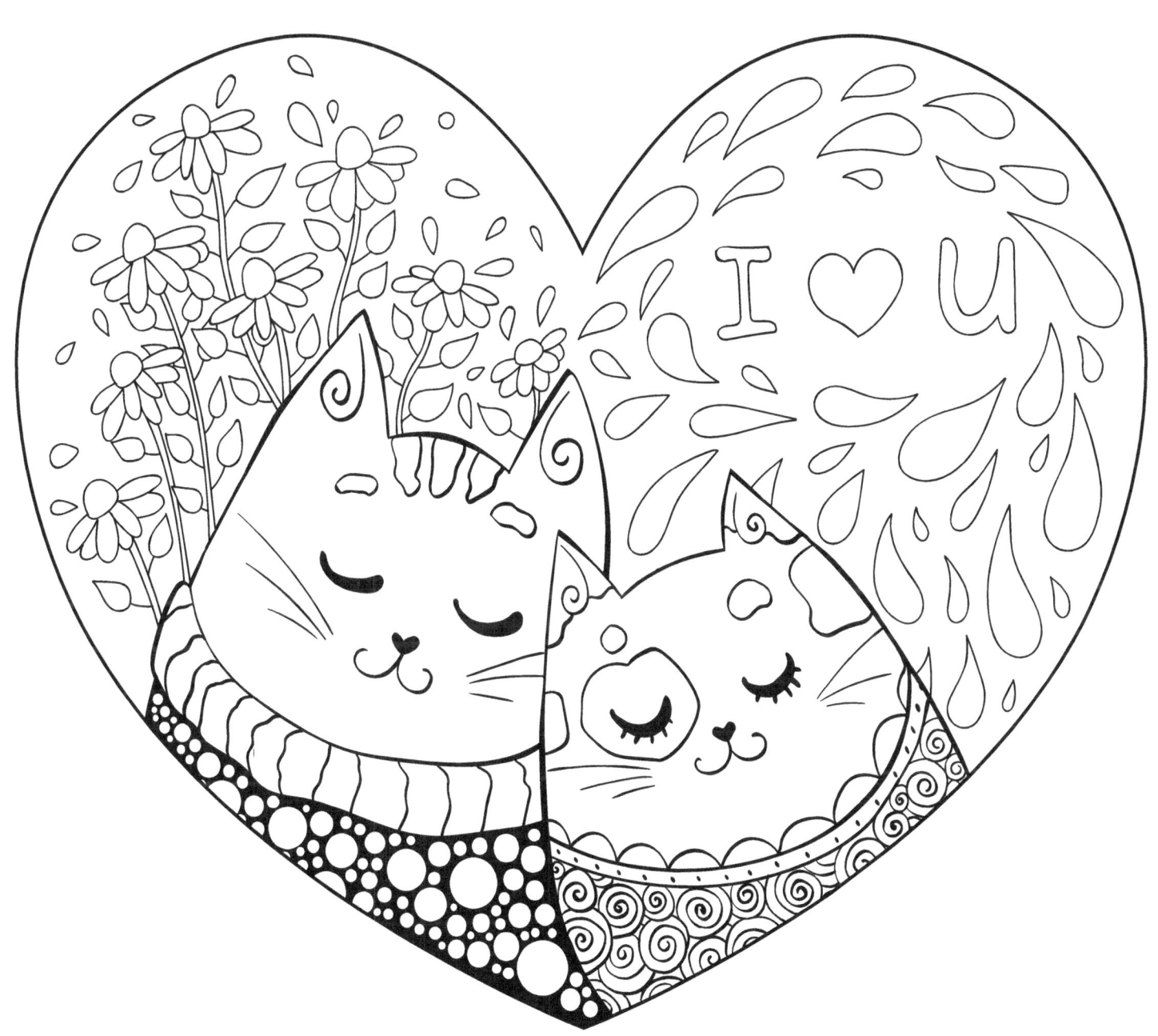

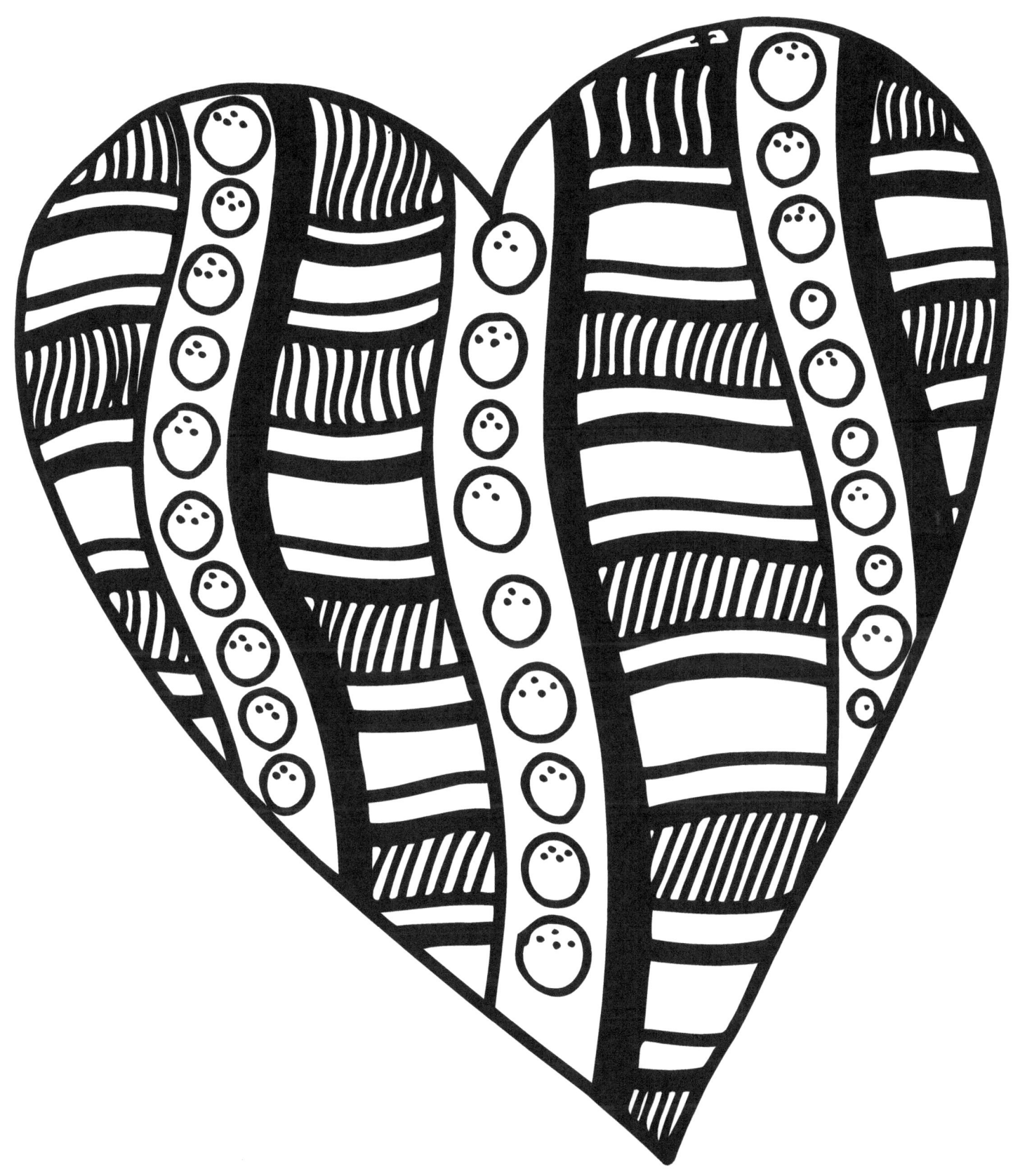

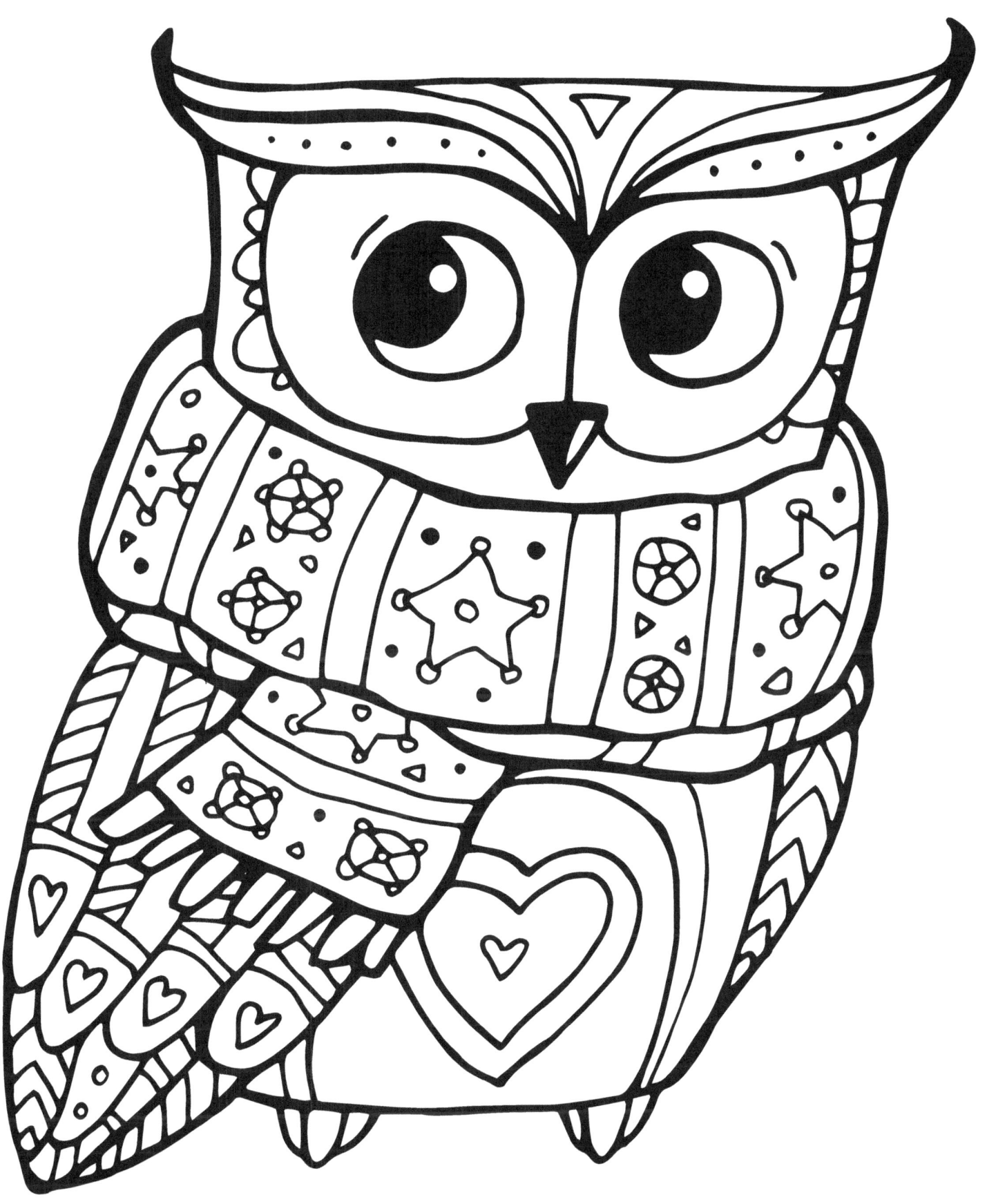

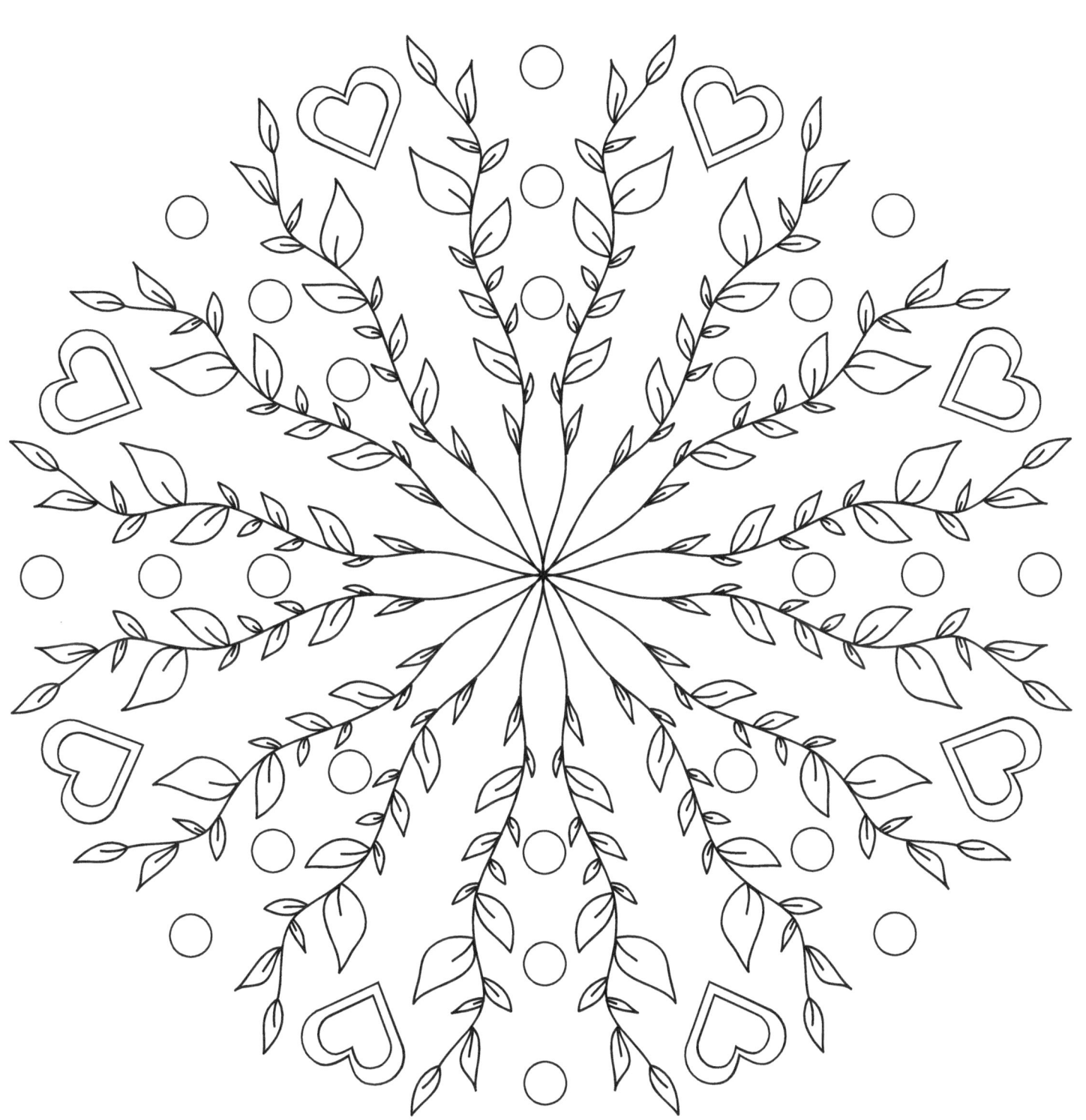

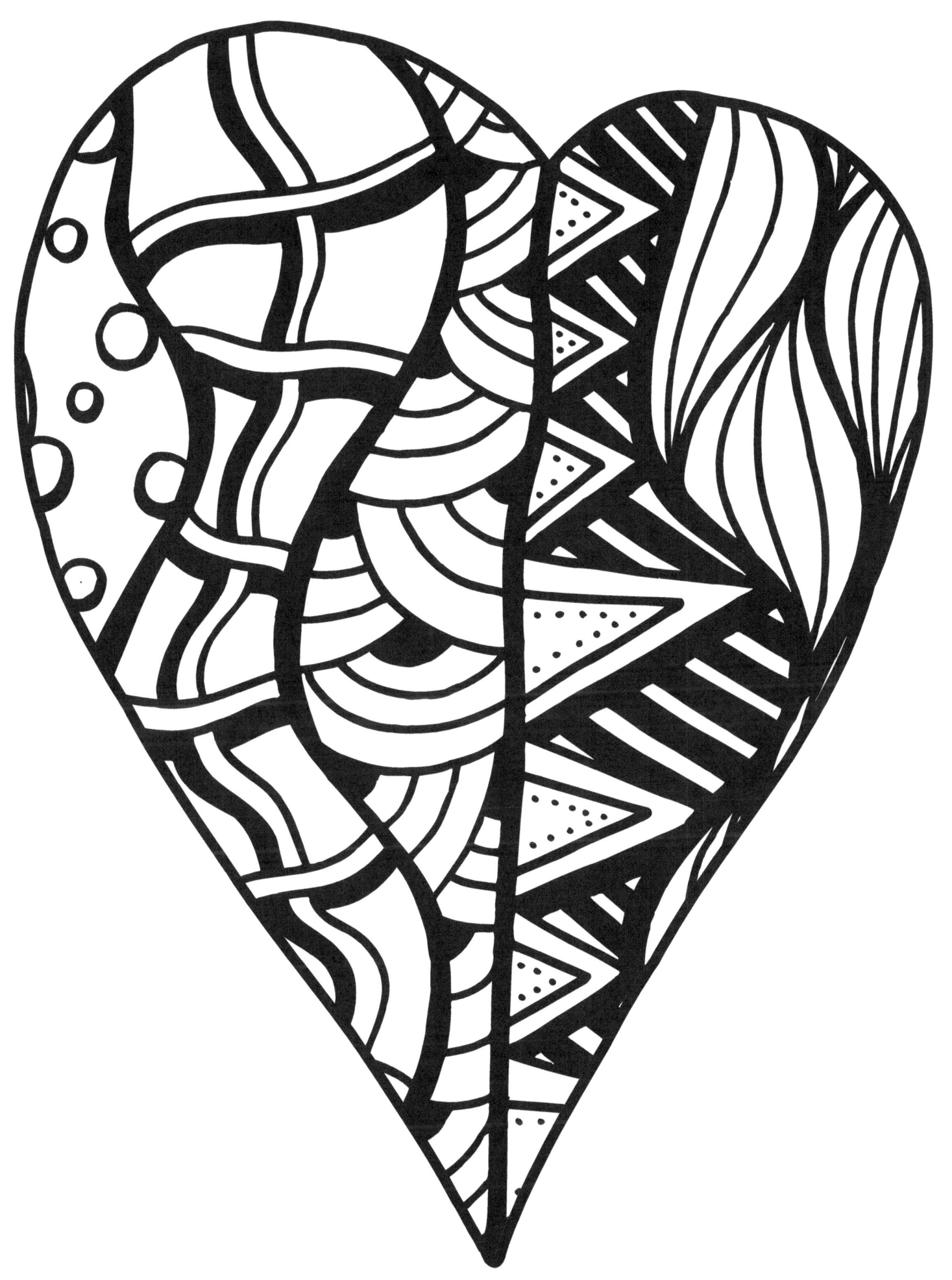

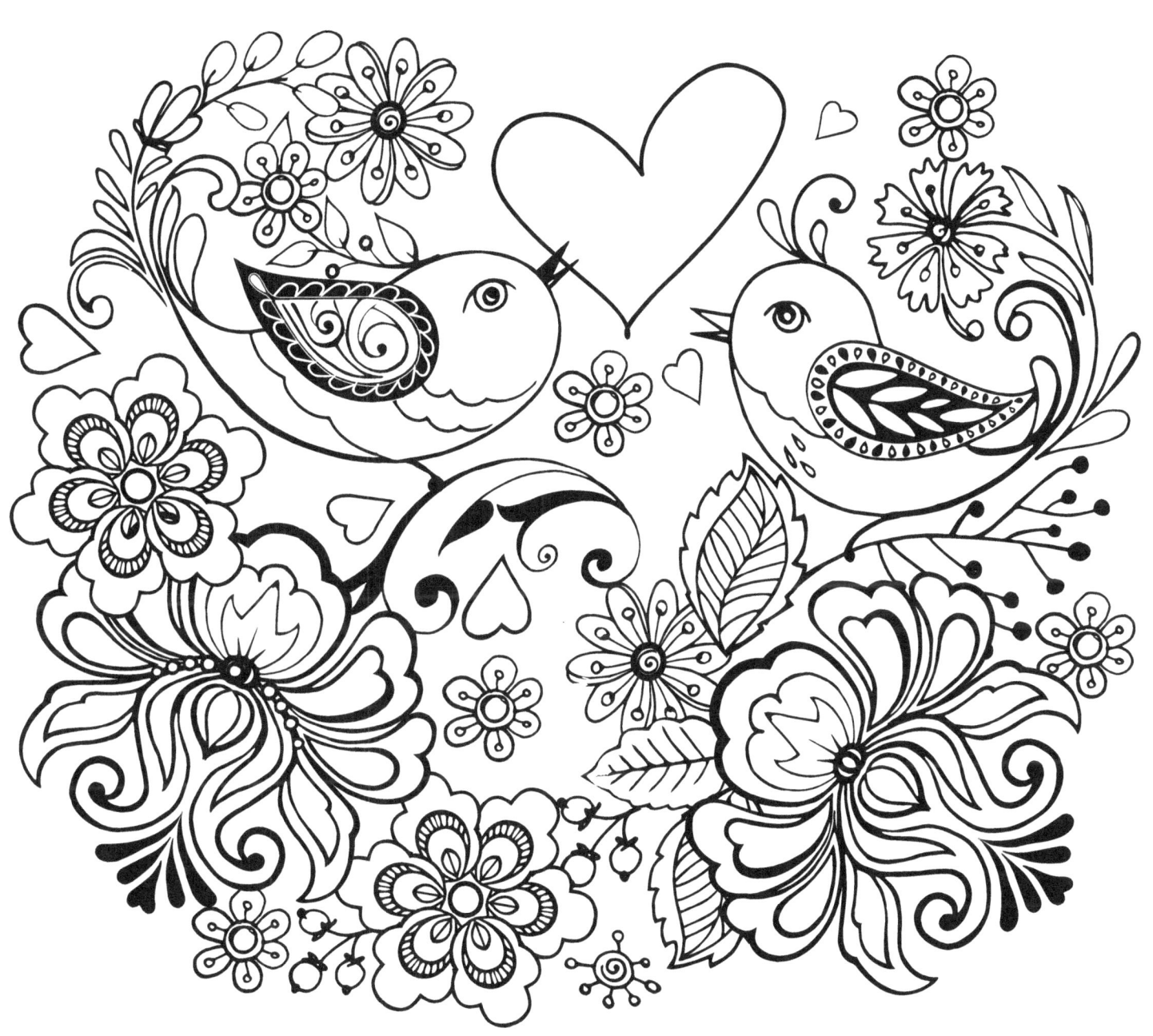

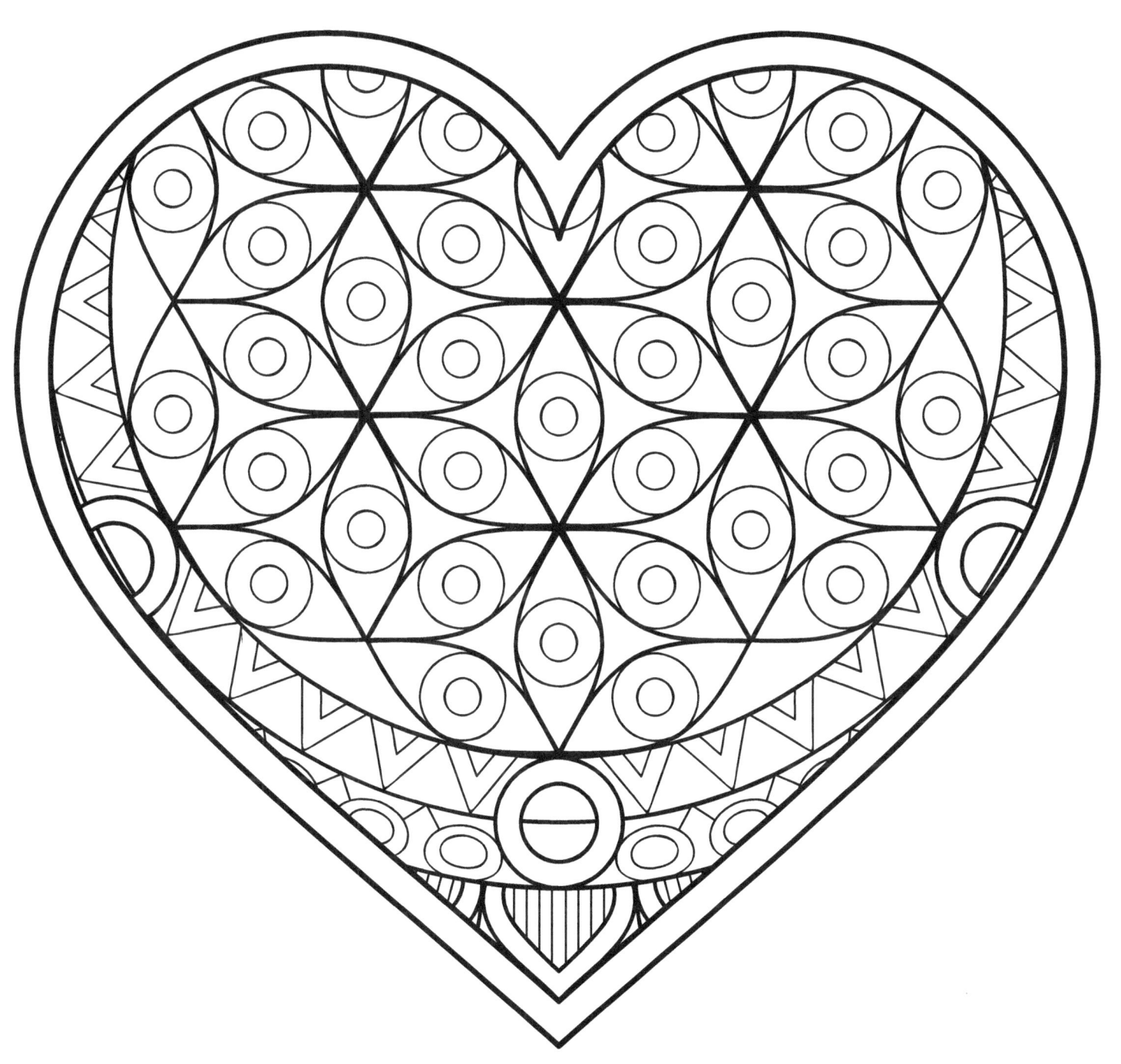

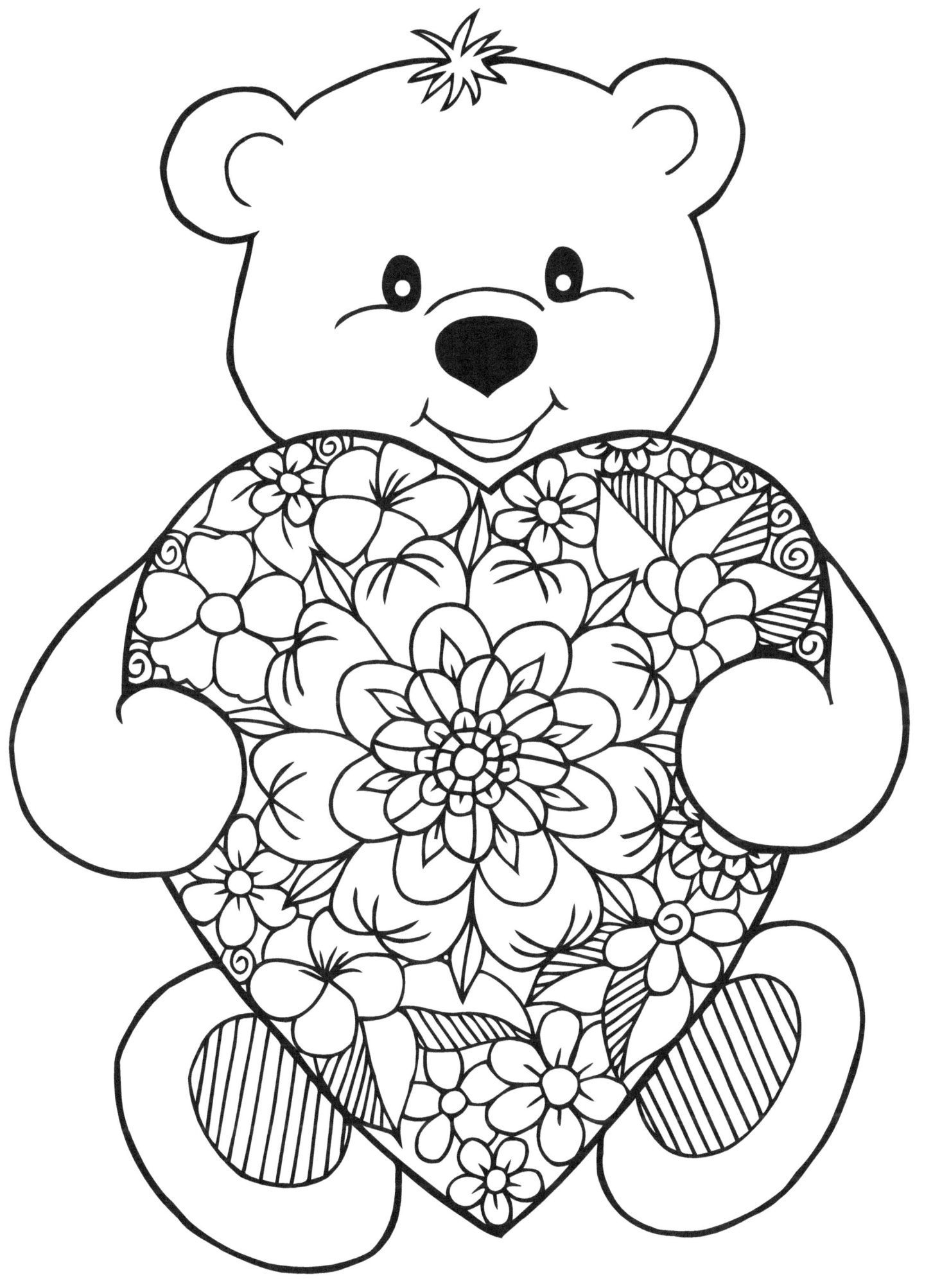

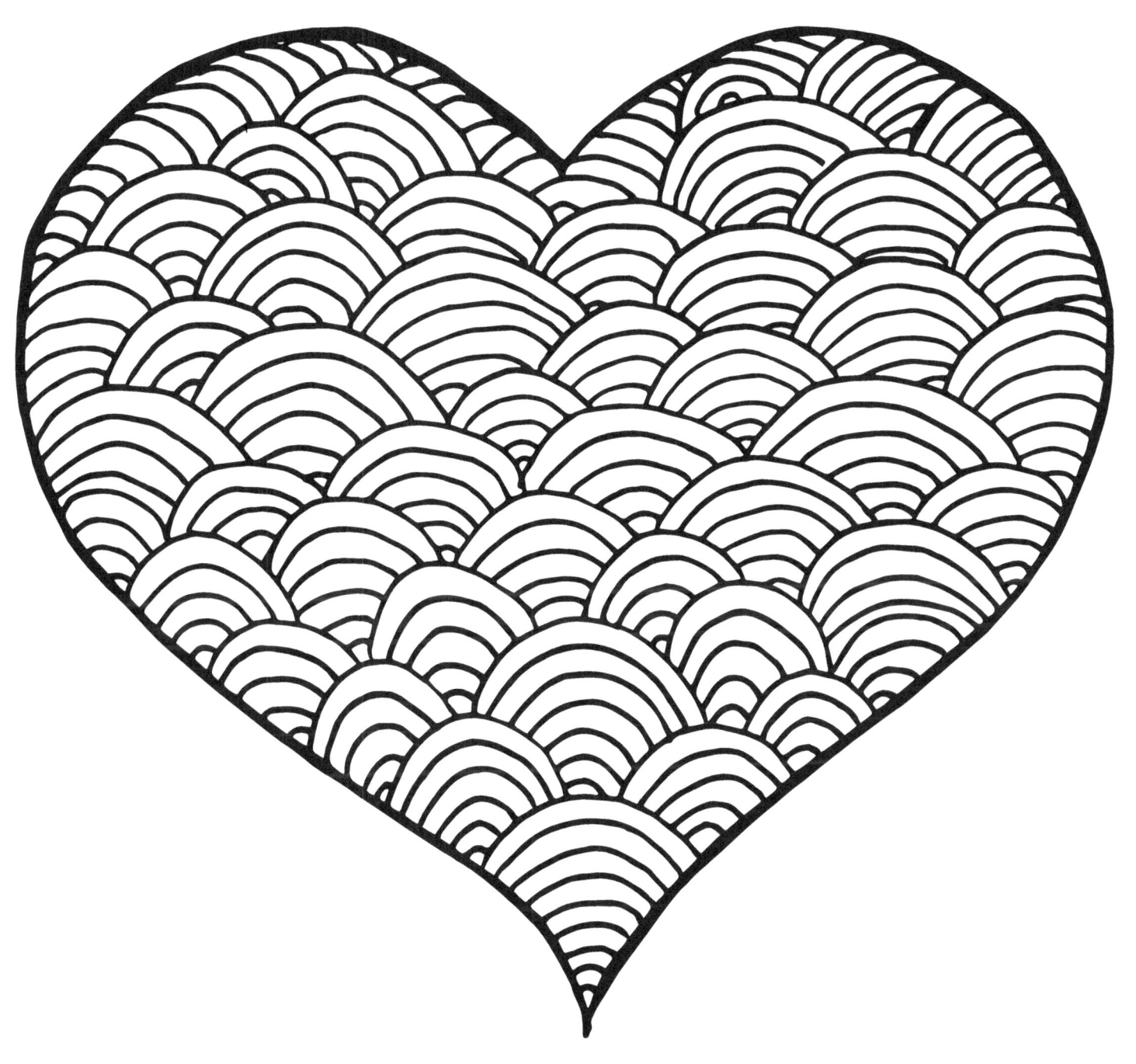

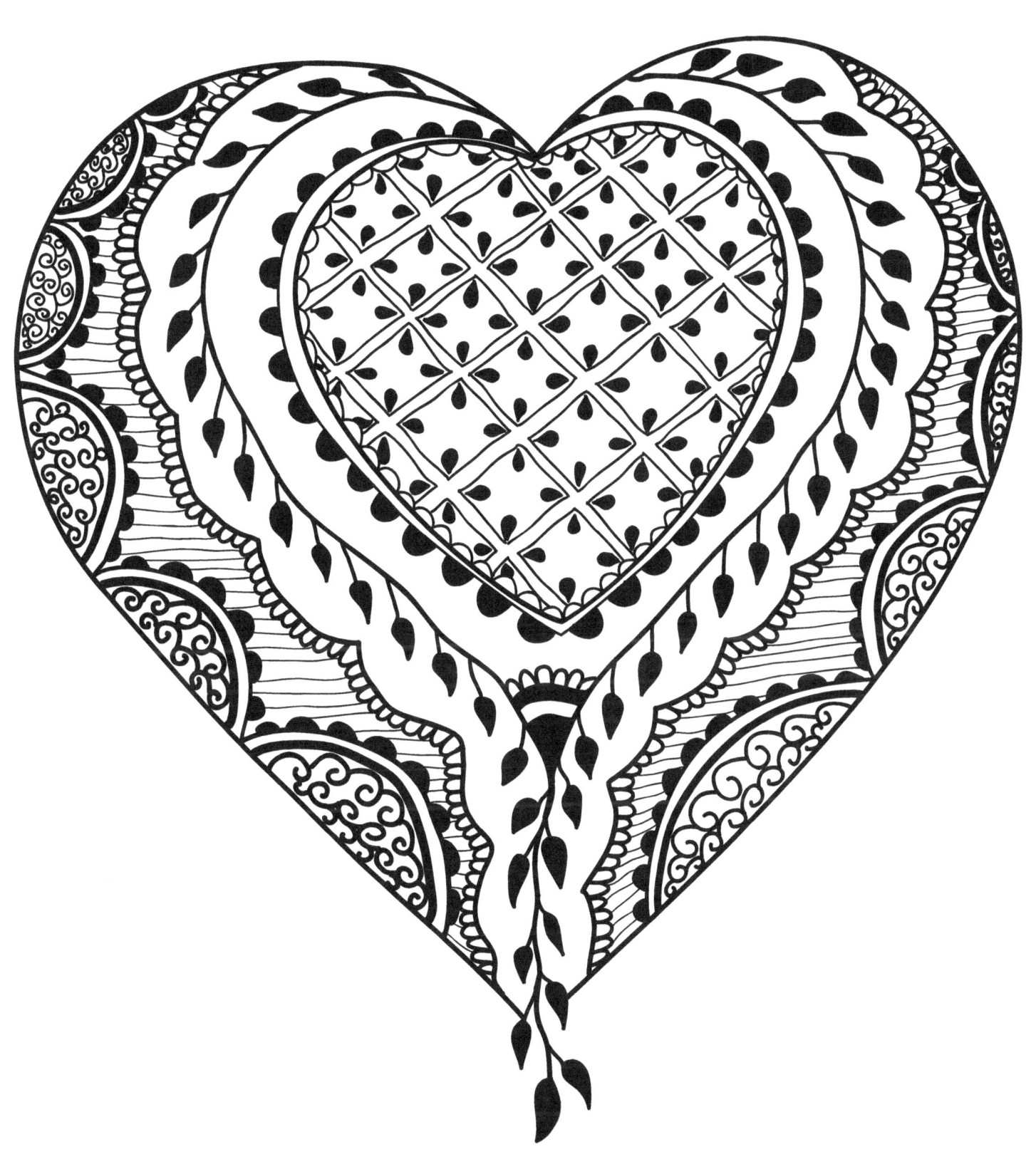

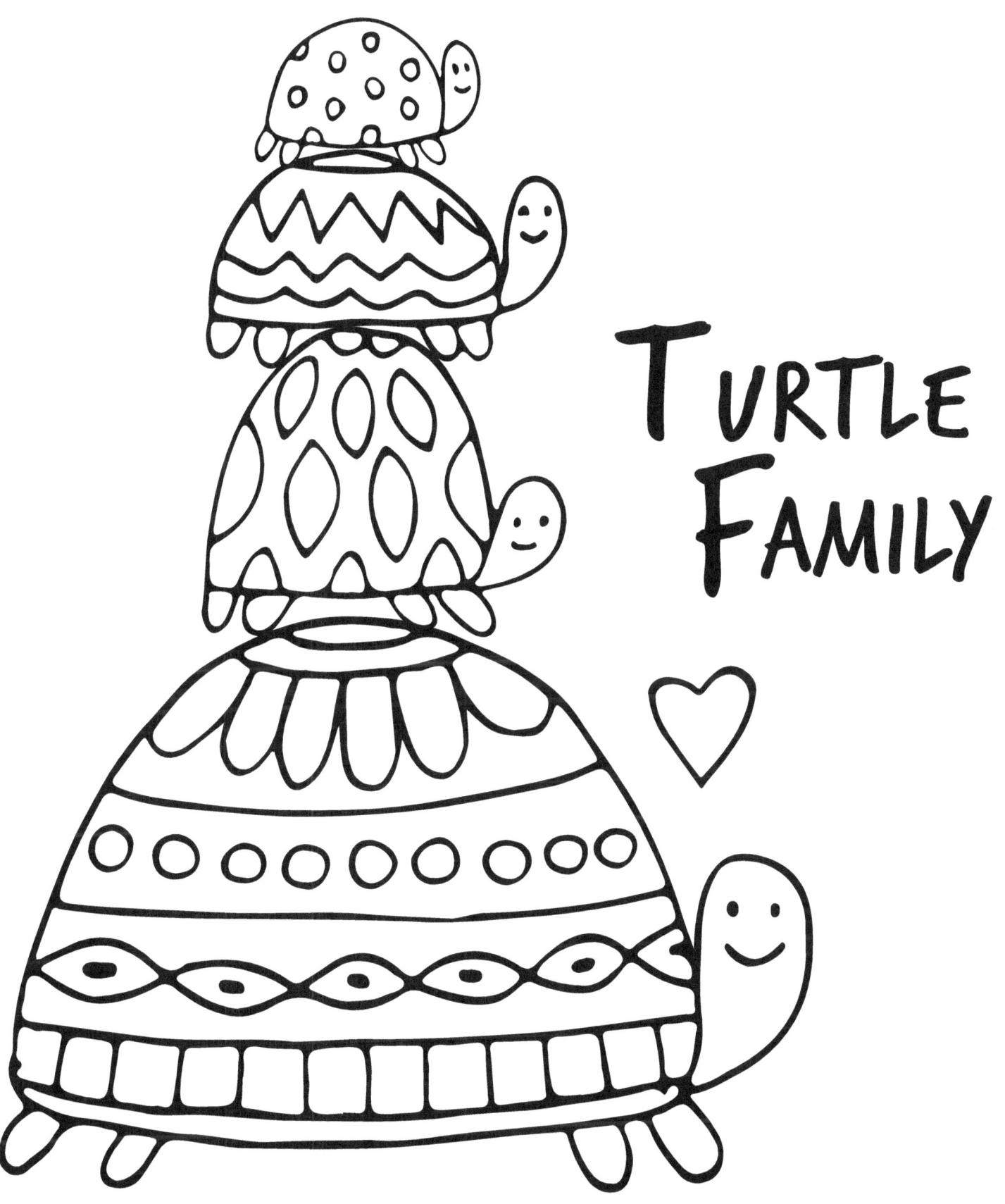

TURTLE
FAMILY

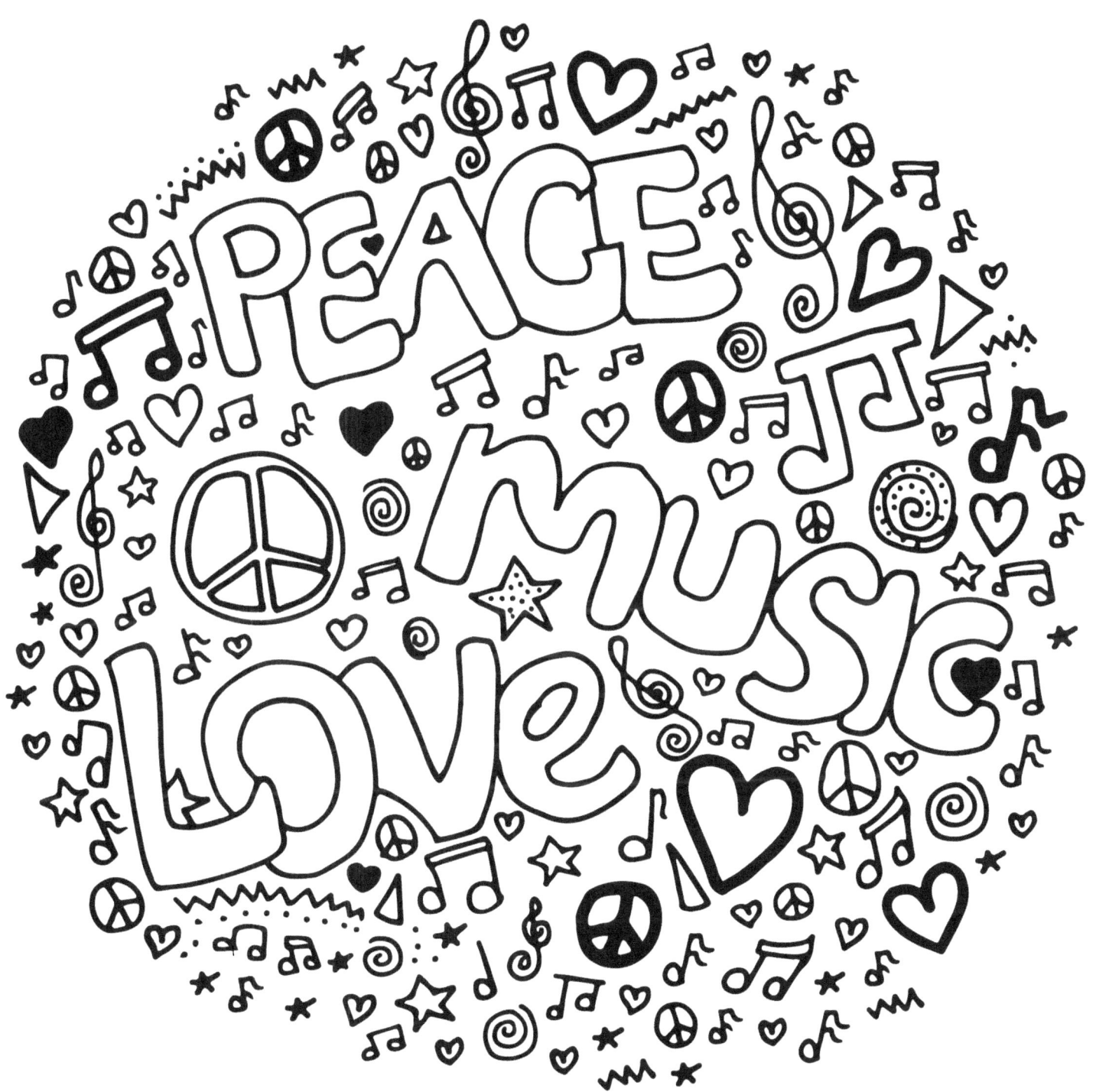

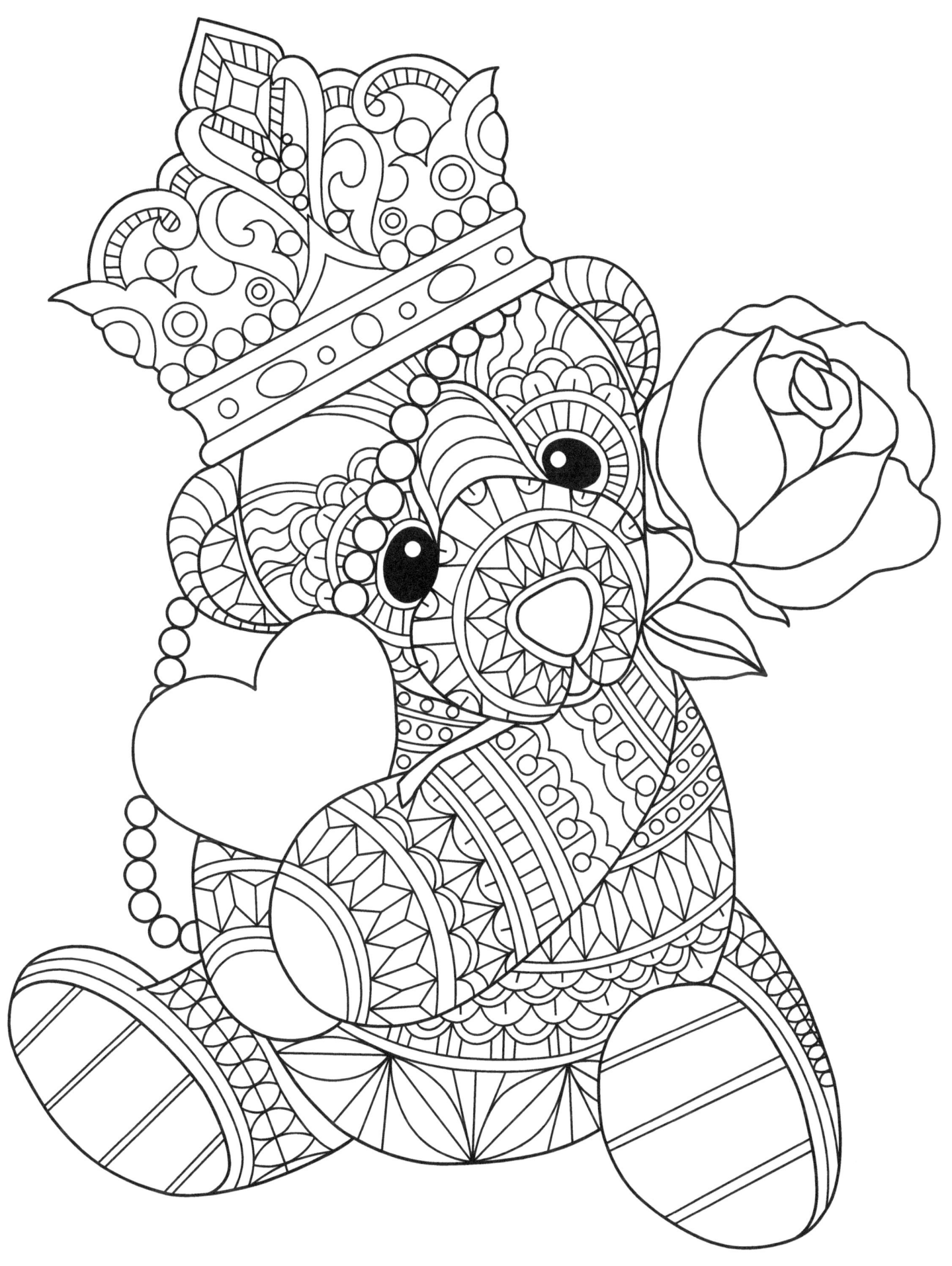

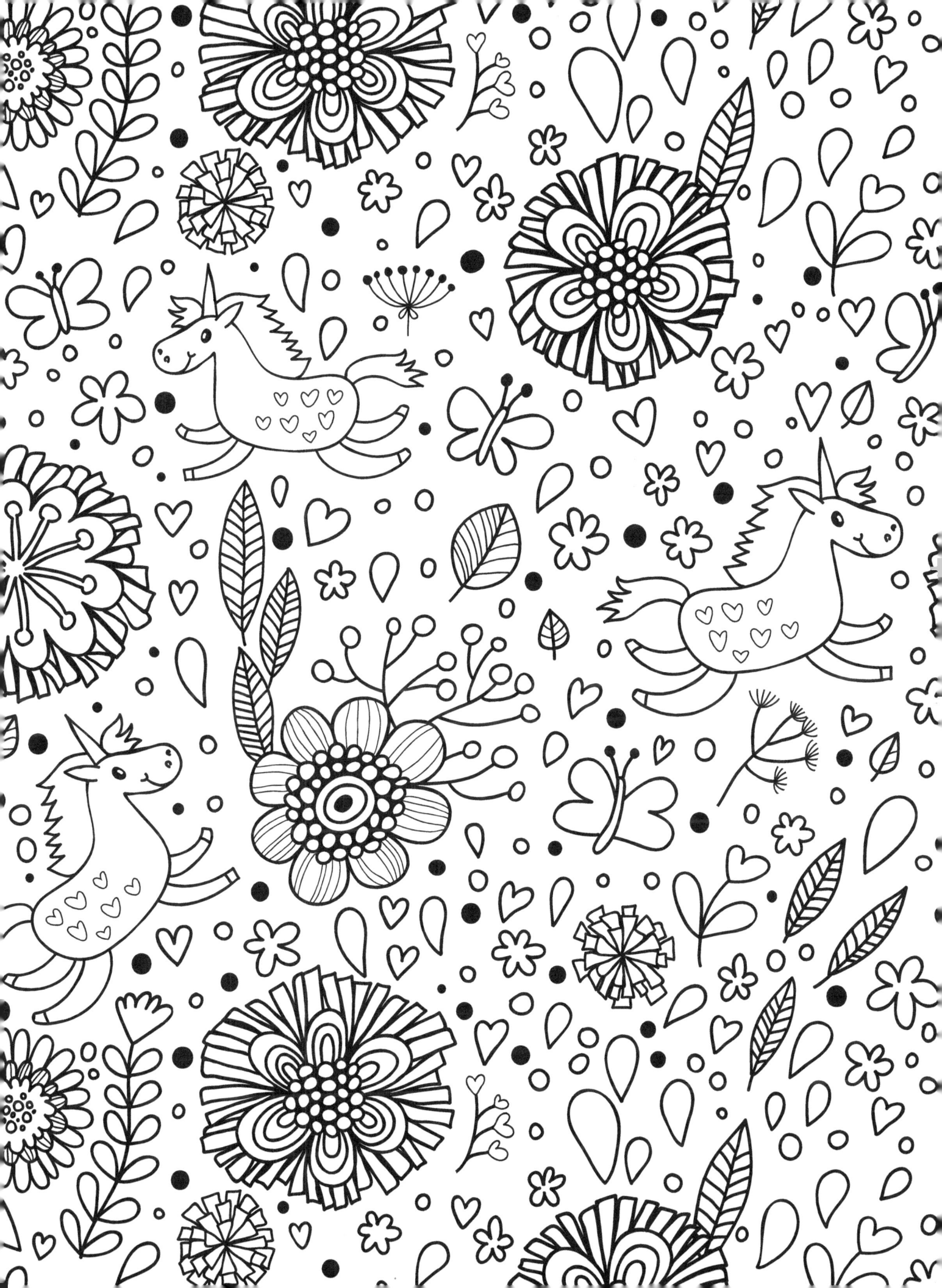

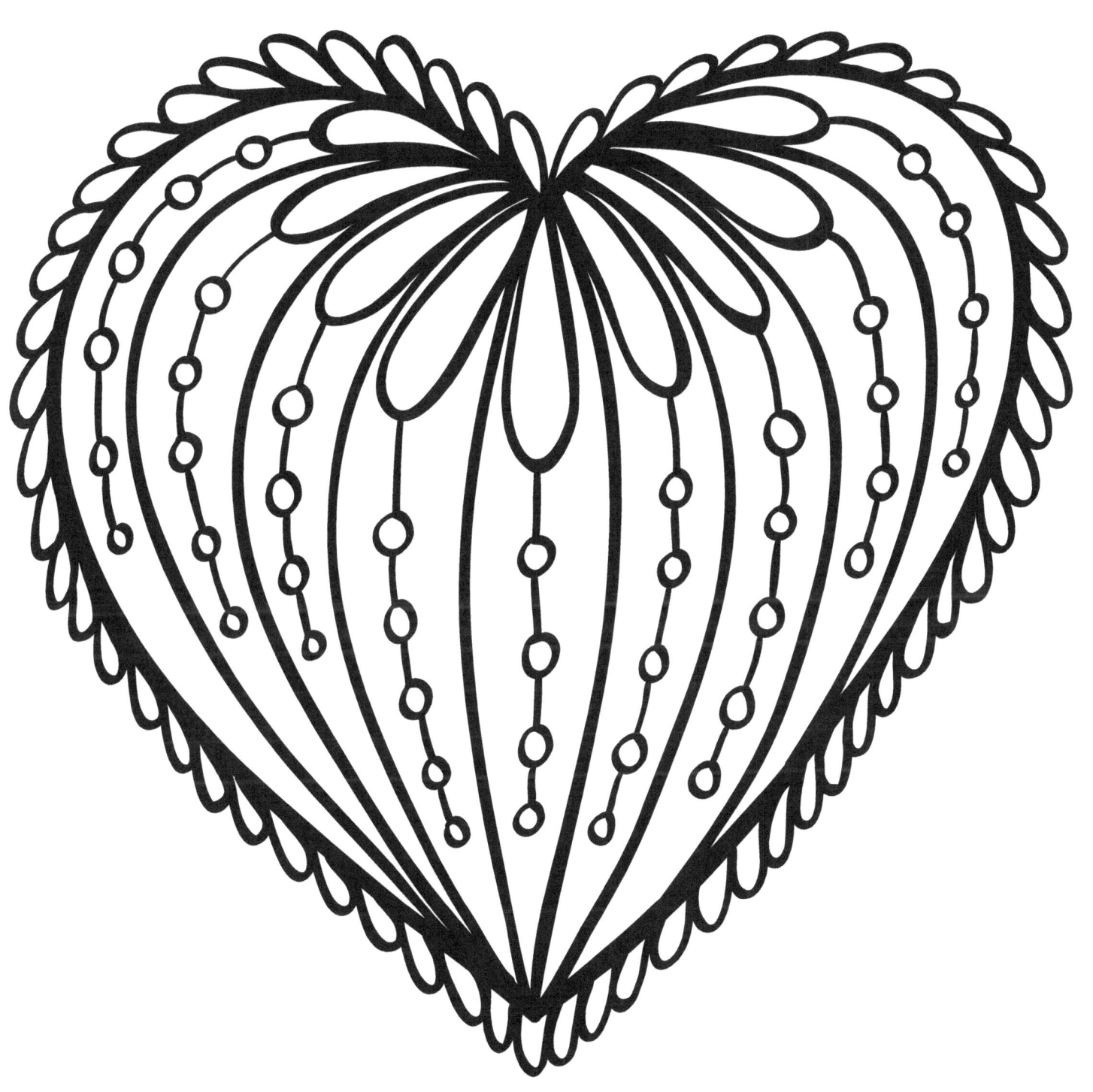

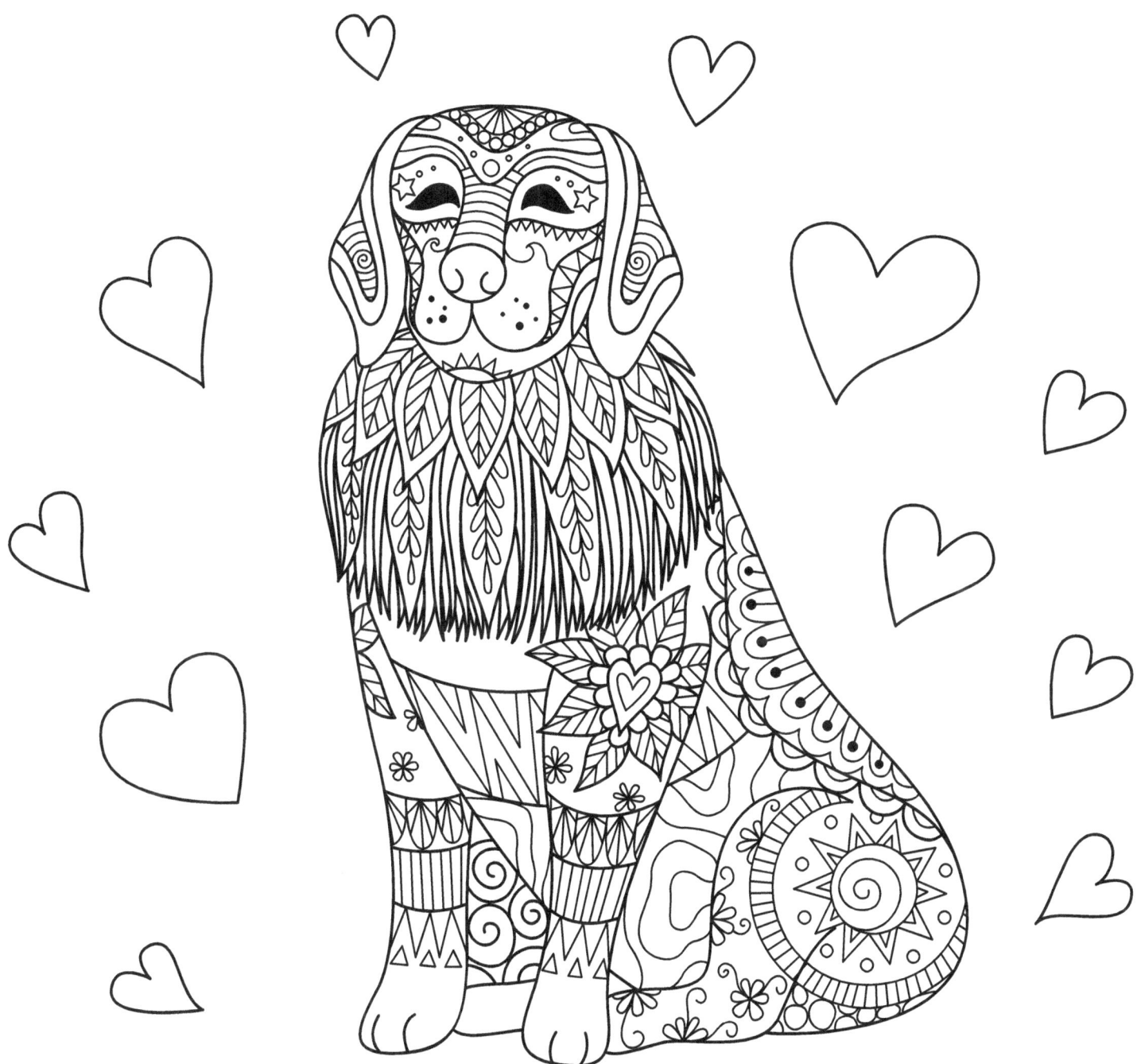

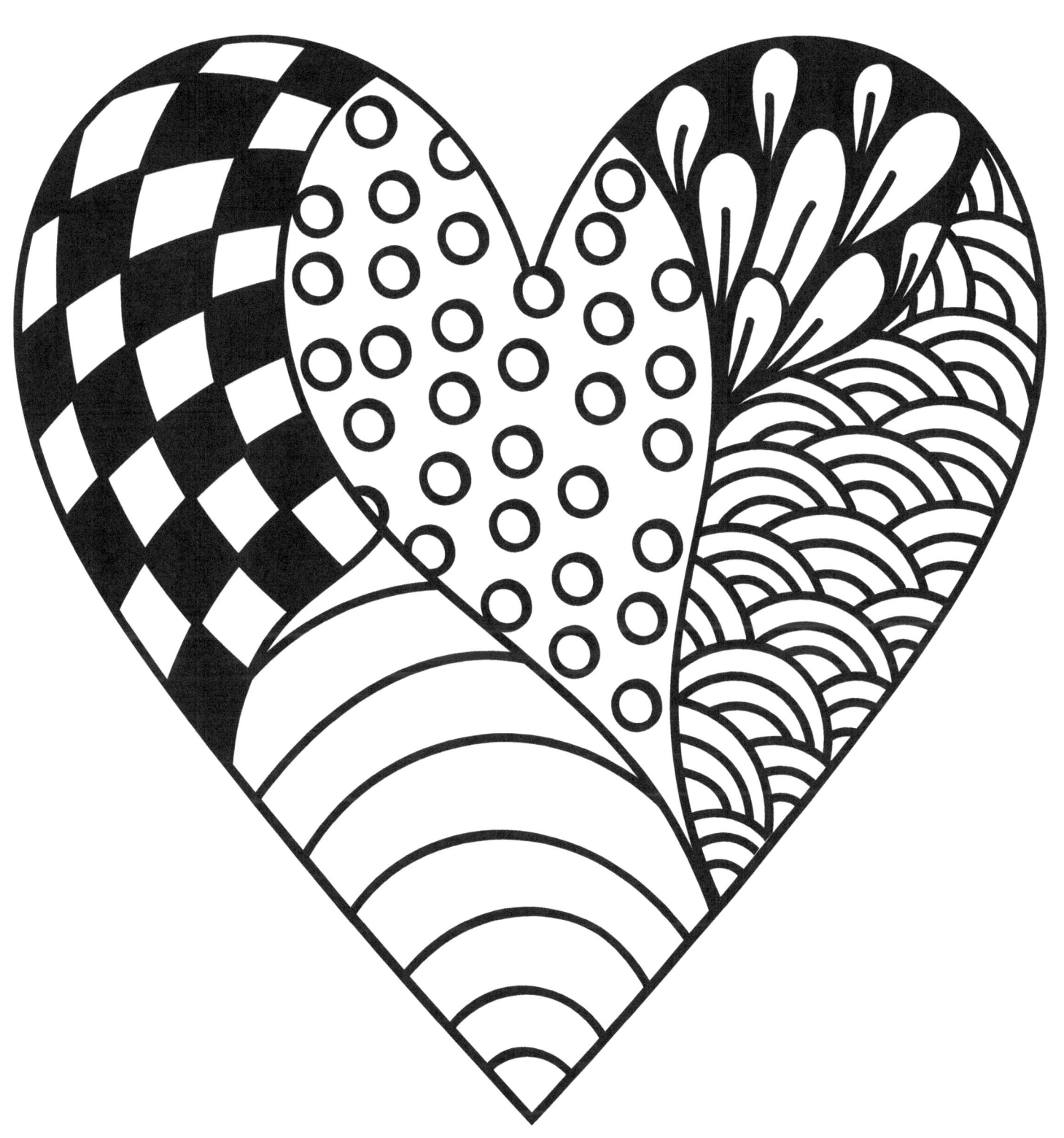

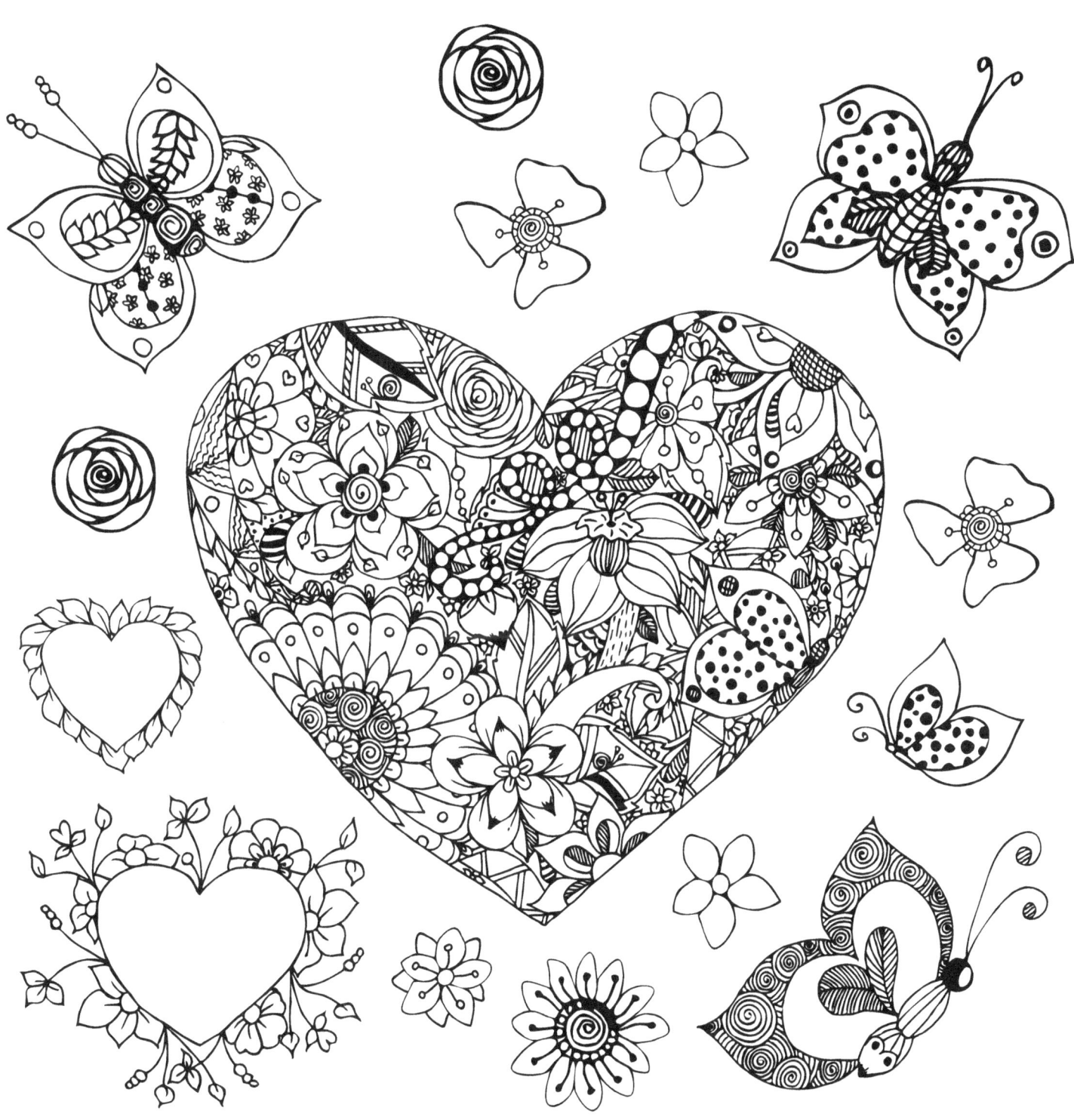

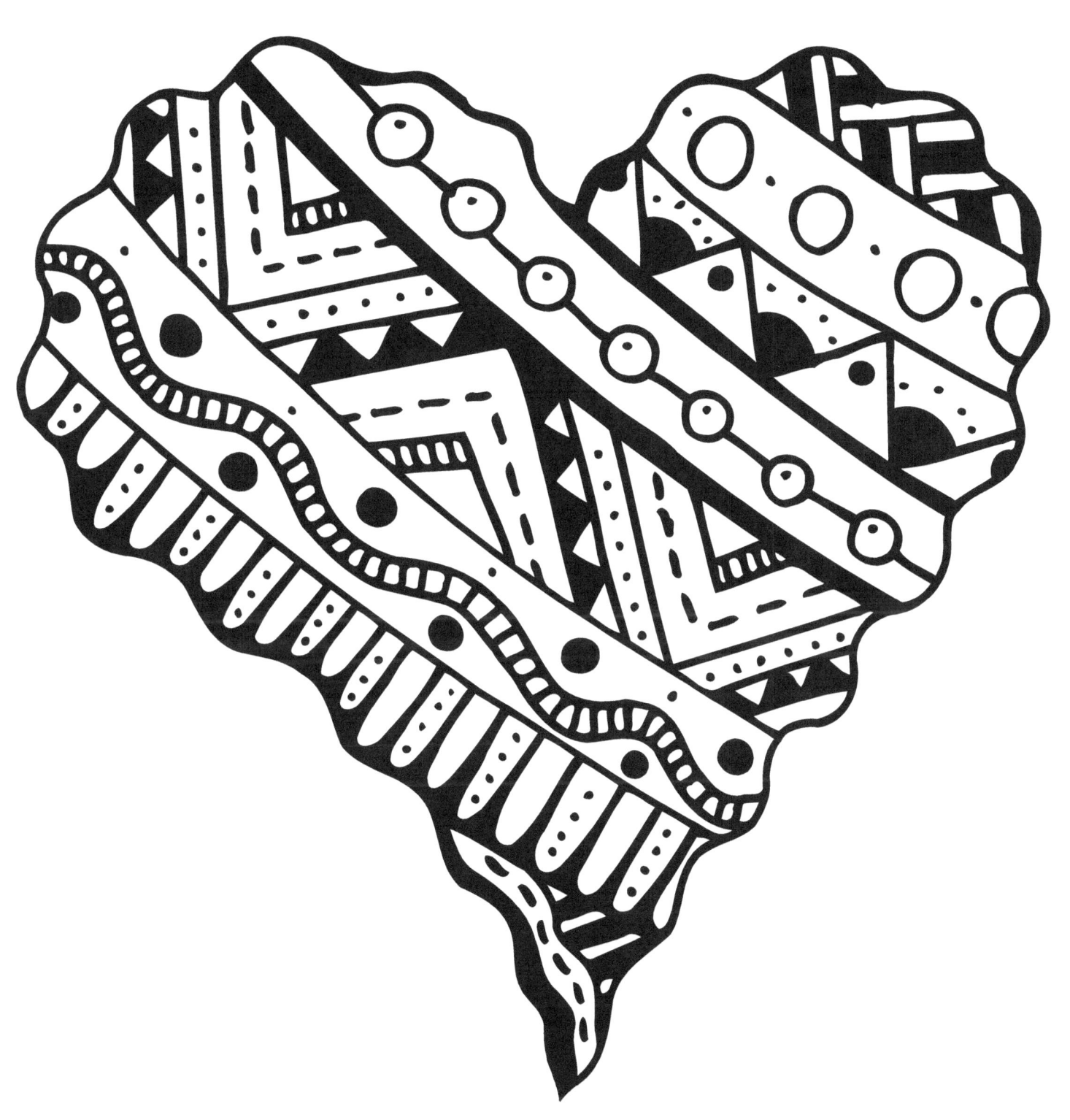

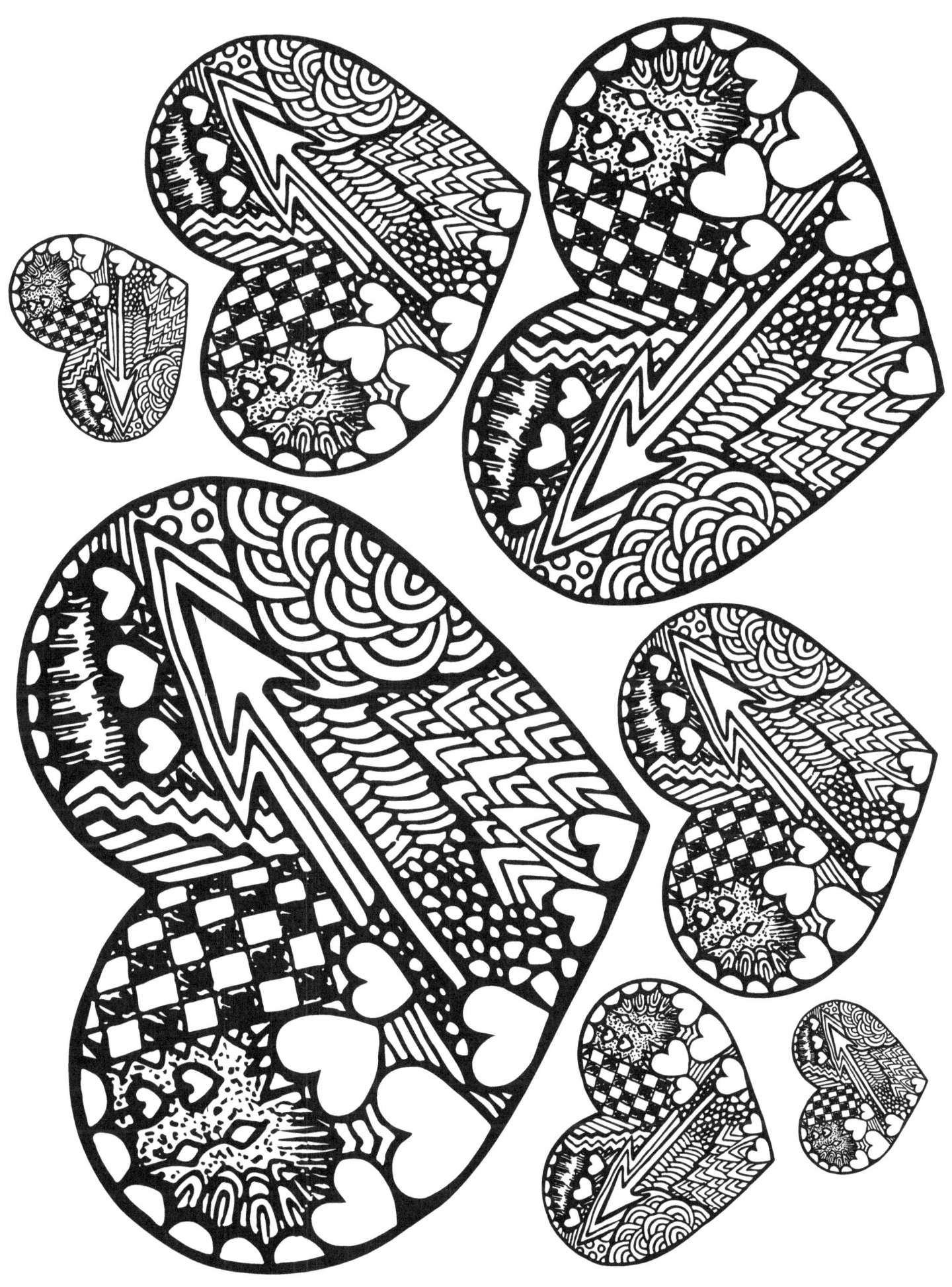

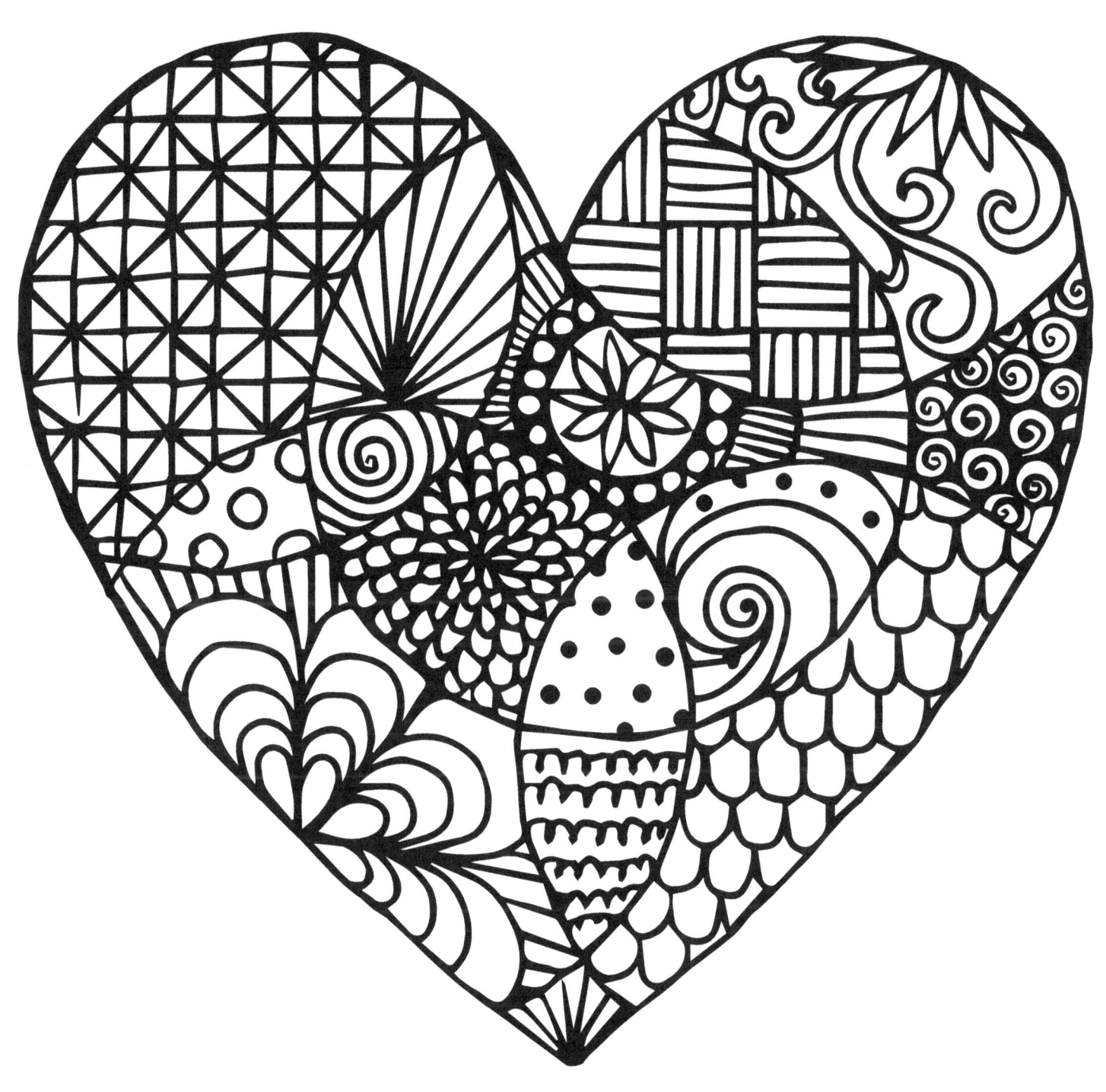

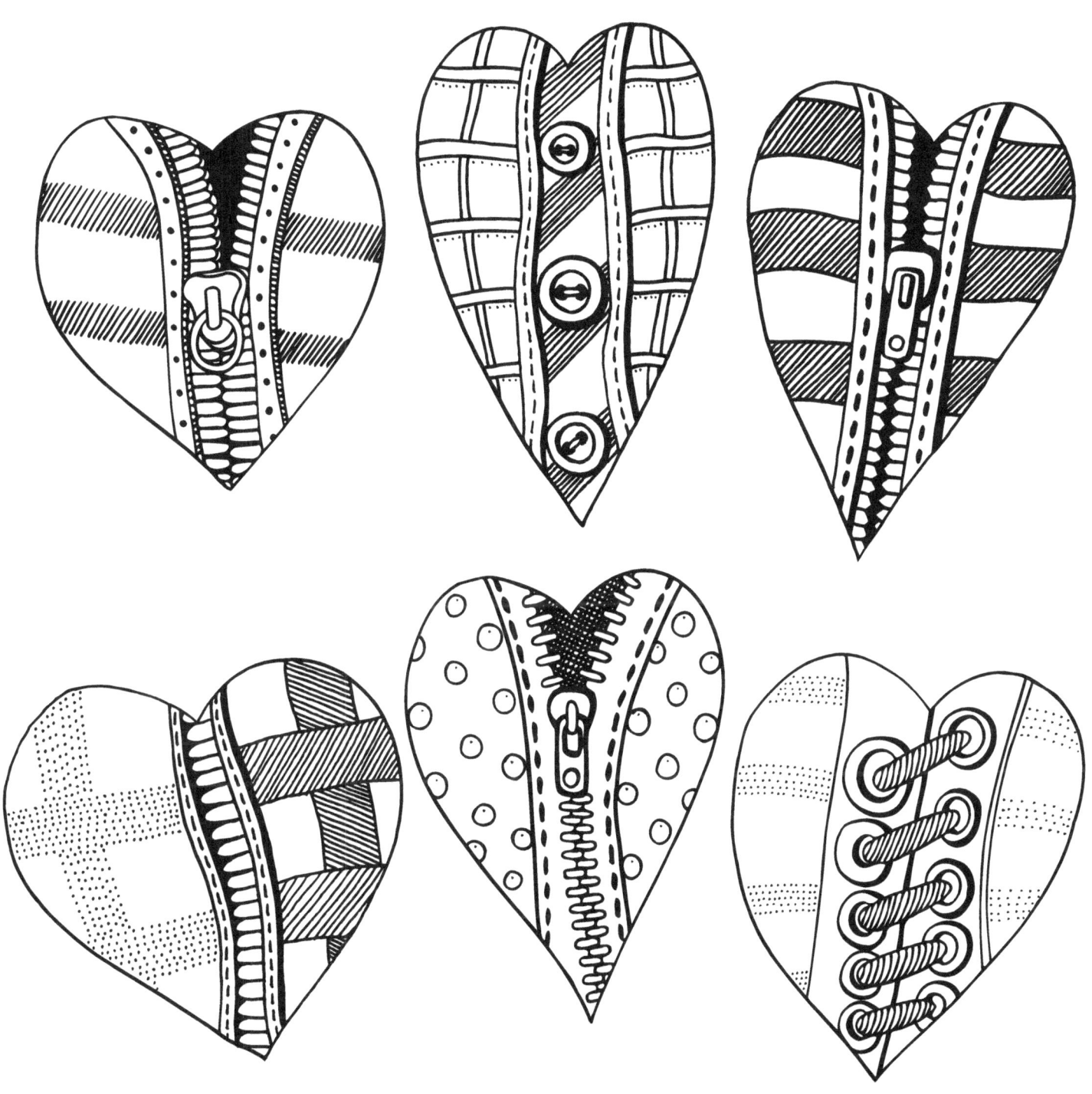

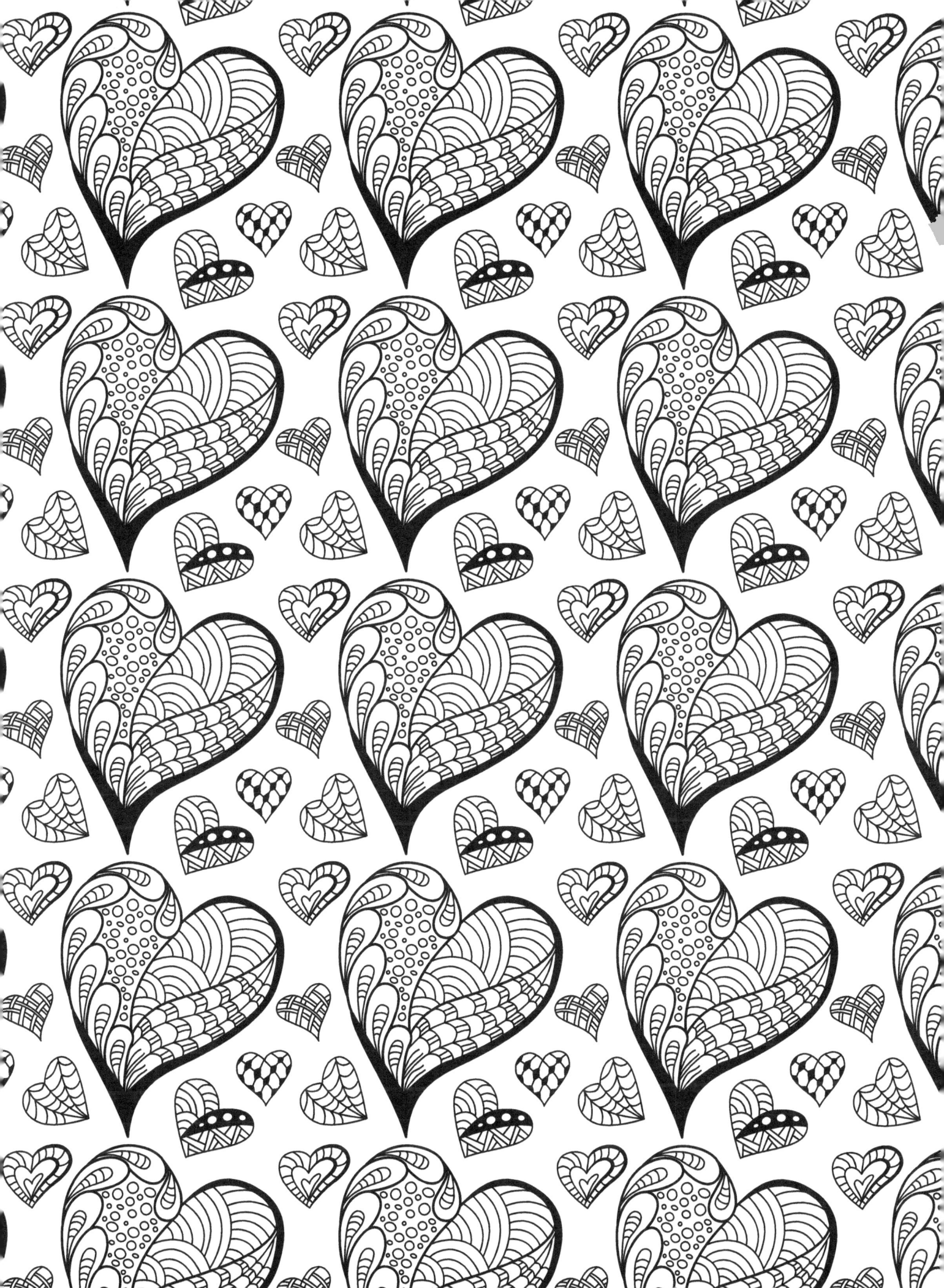

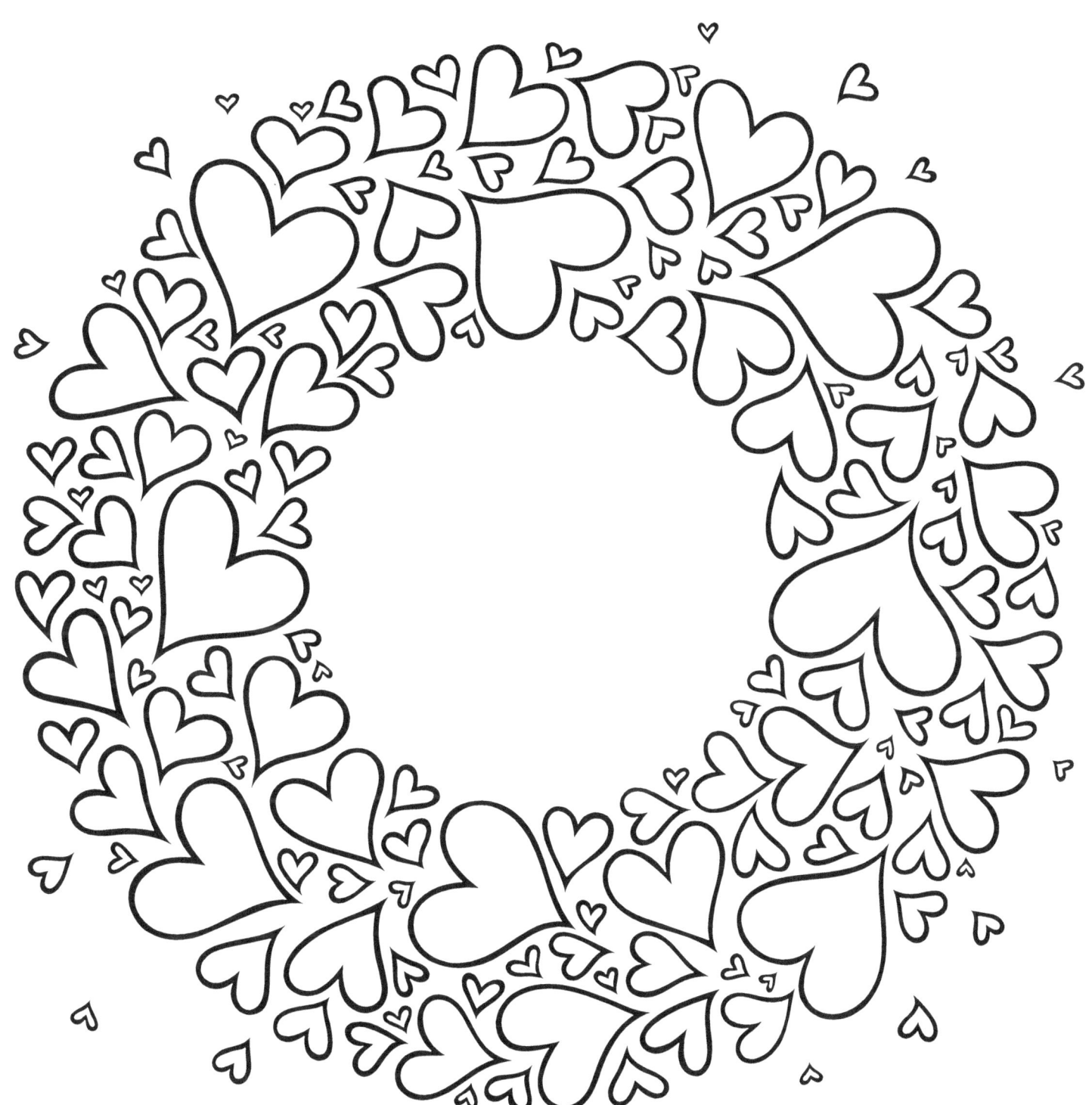

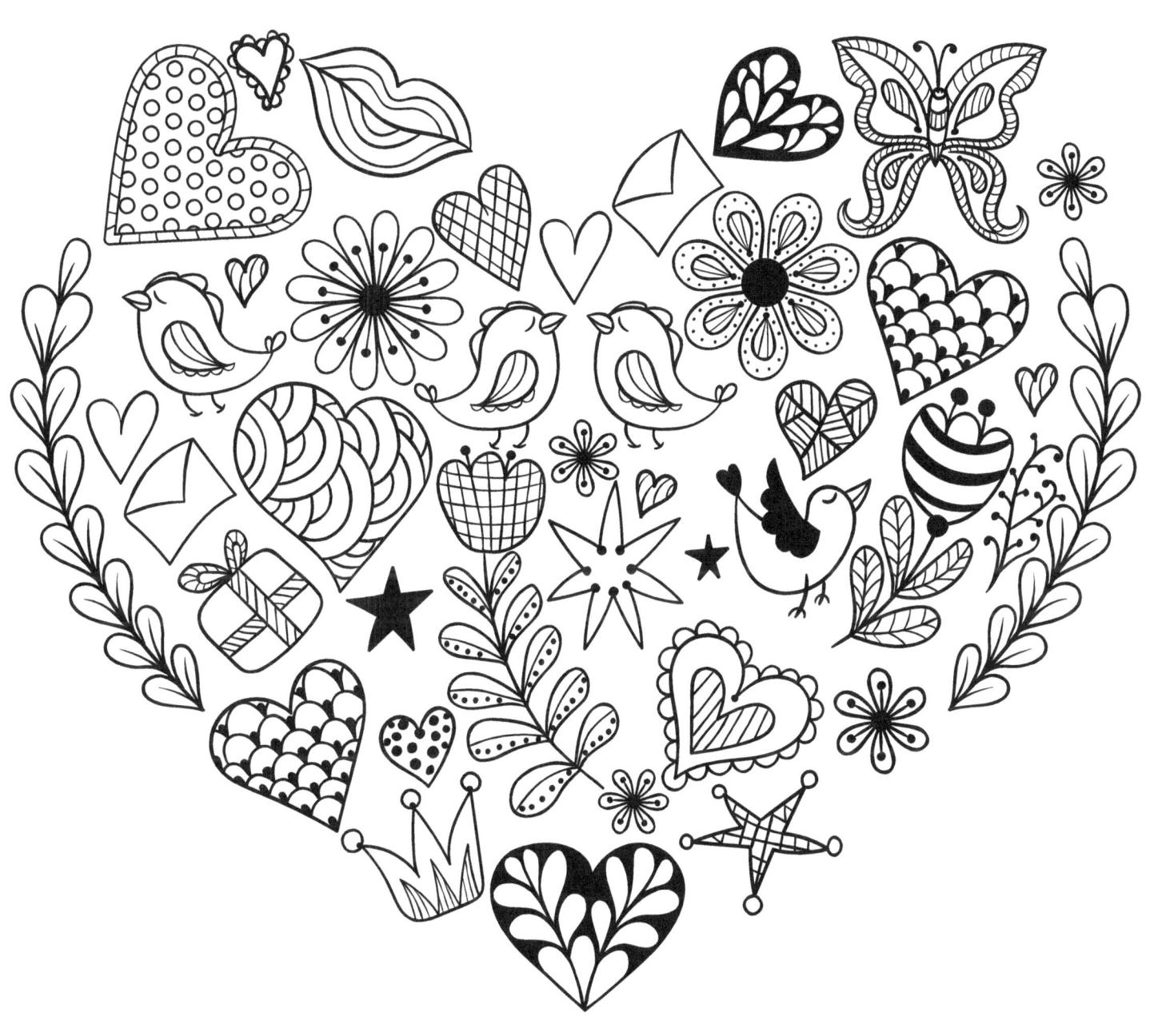

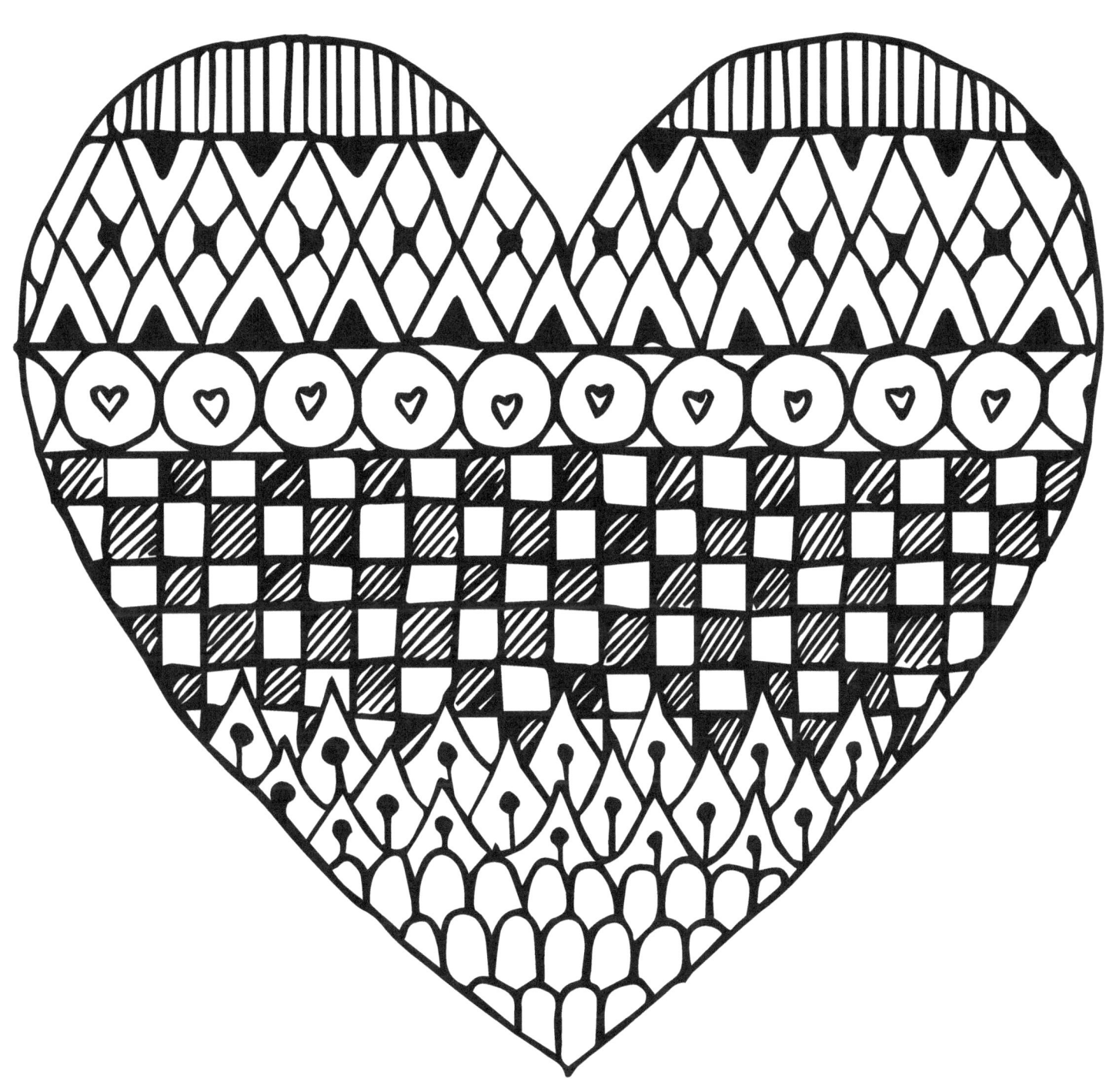

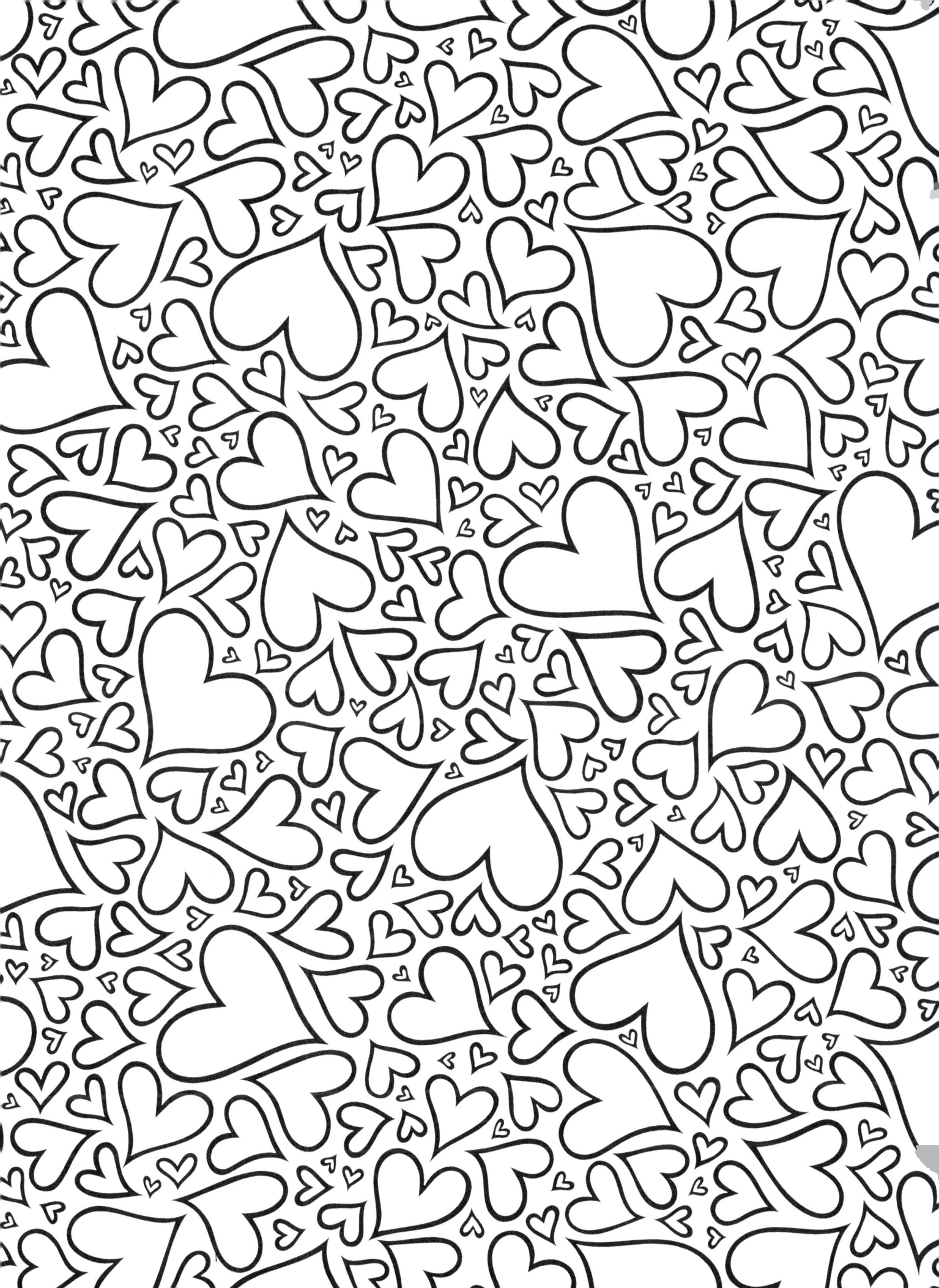

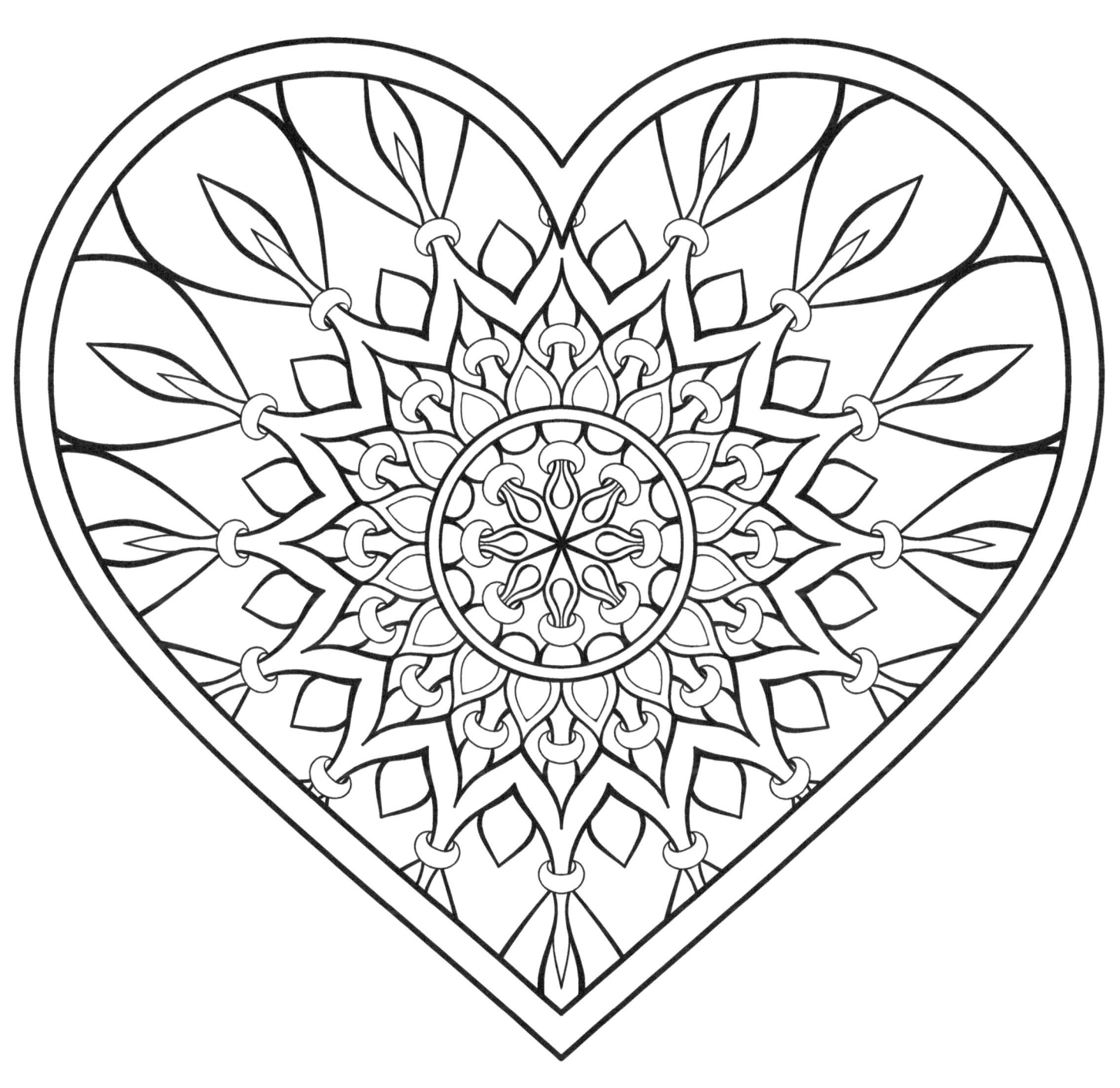

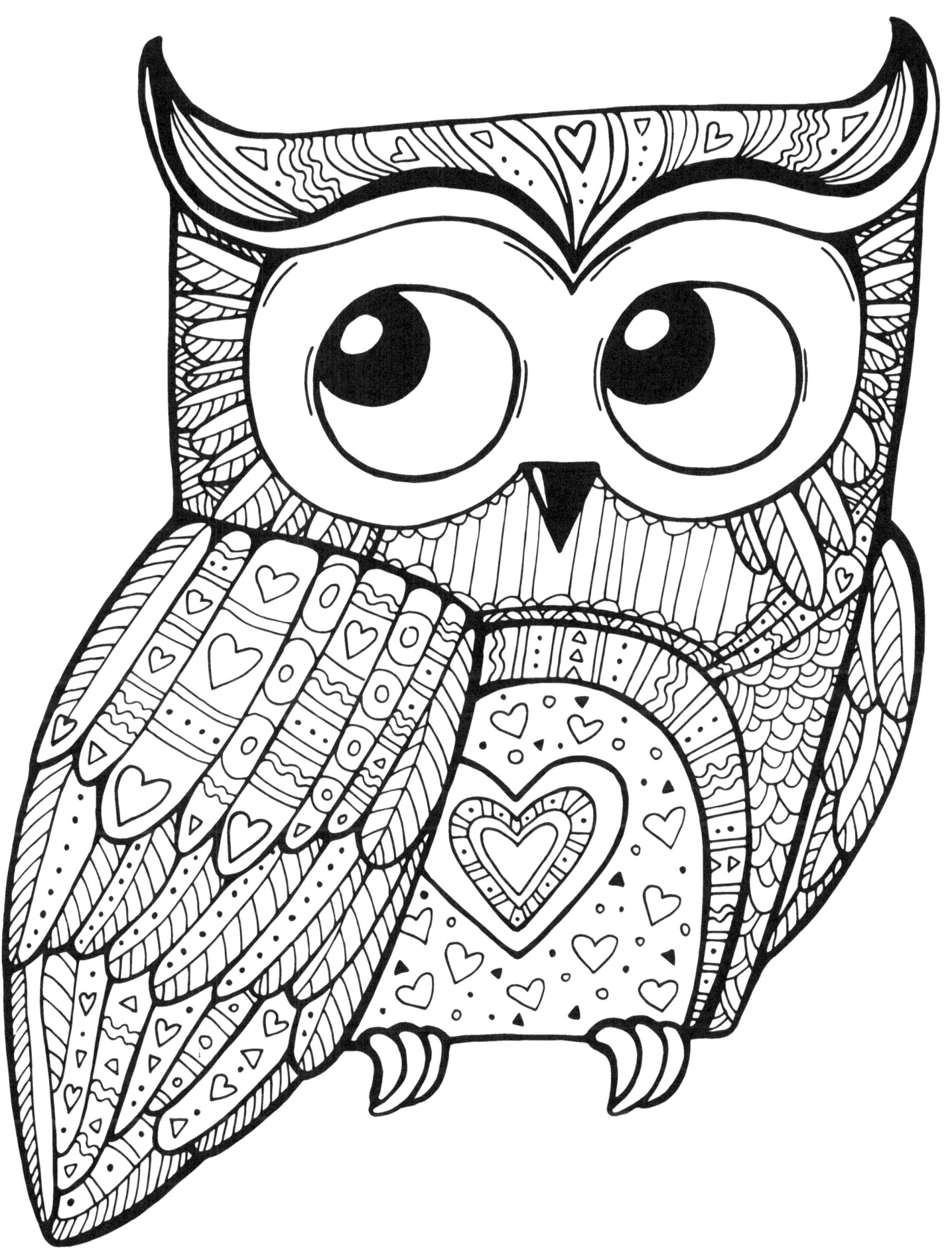

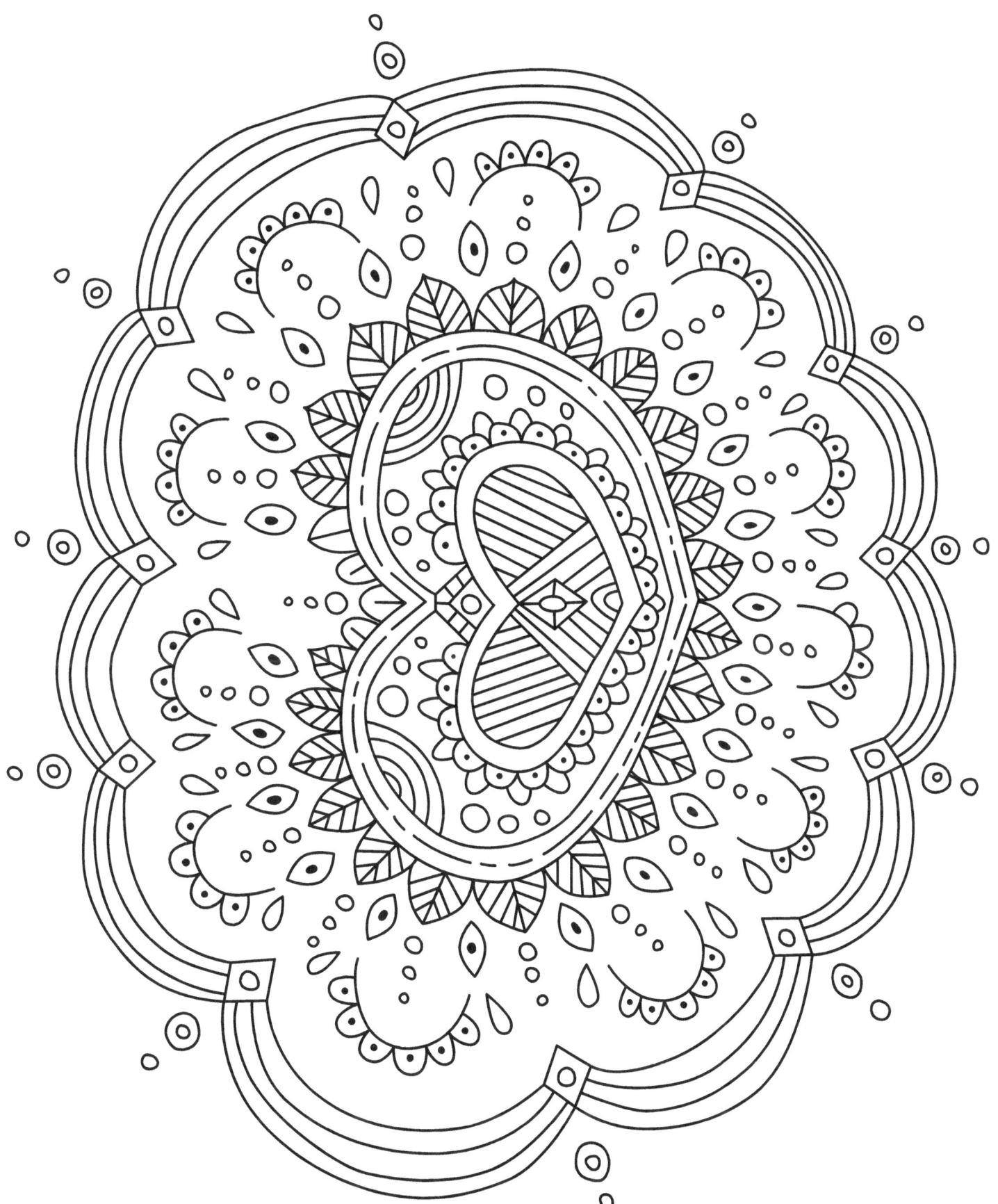

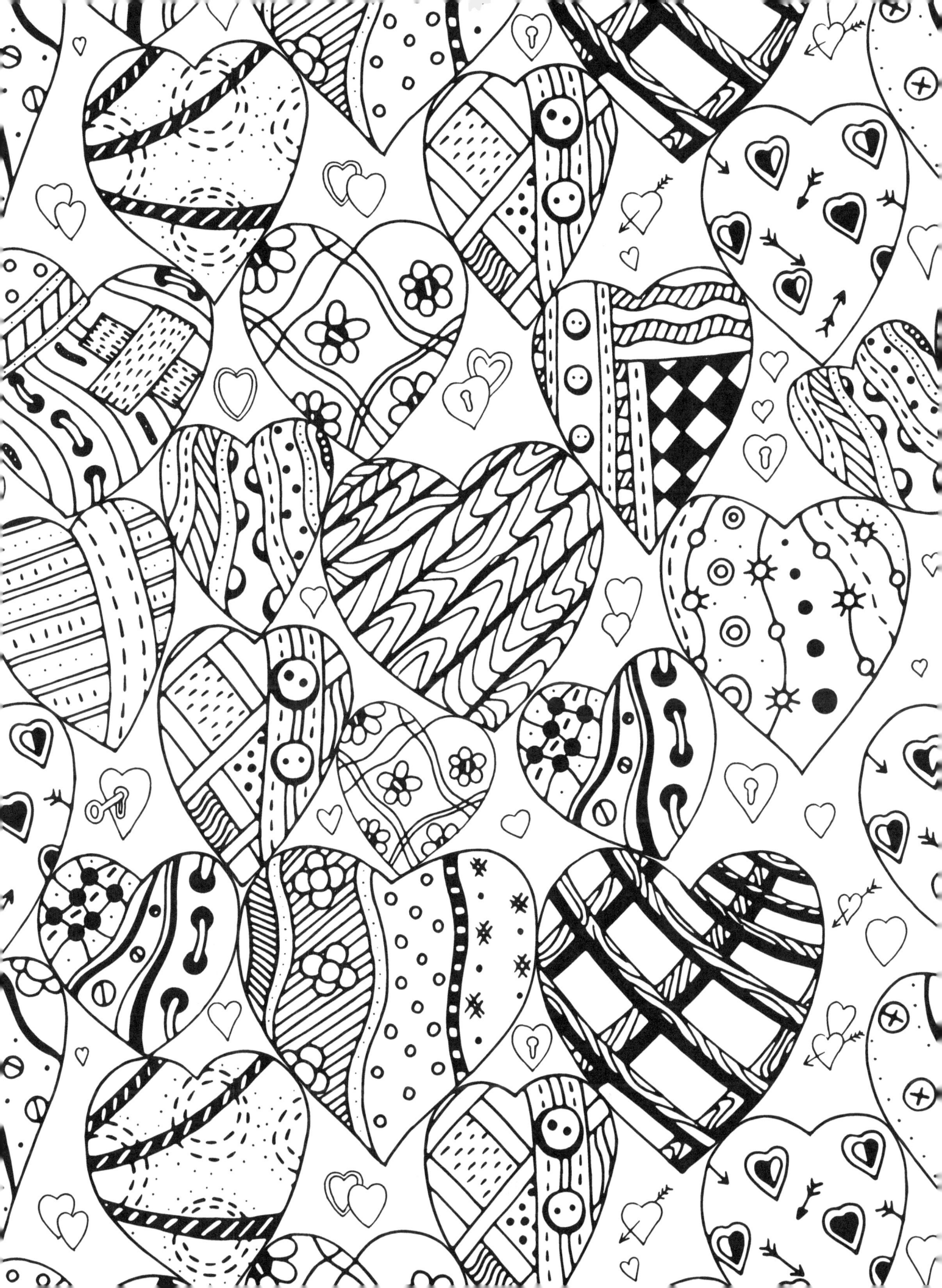

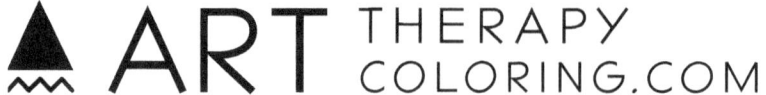

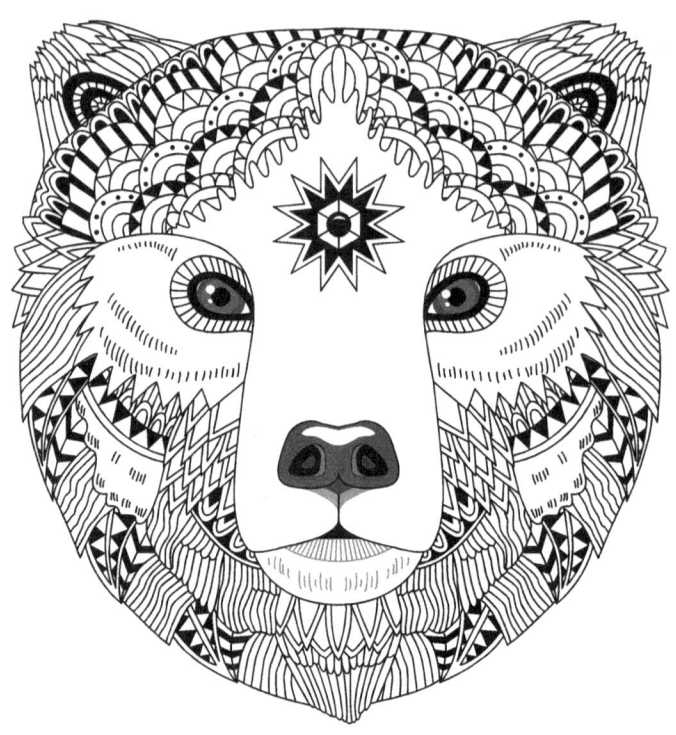

Did You Enjoy Our Coloring Book?

We Want To Hear About It!

Help spread the word about our coloring books! The best way to spread the word is through reviews. We know how busy you are, especially with all of that coloring, but we would appreciate it!

Visit our website at www.arttherapycoloring.com

Over 200 Art Therapy Coloring Books

See our collection of over 200 Art Therapy Coloring Books for Adults, Men, Women, Seniors, Teens, Kids, Boys, and Girls.

Coloring Books For Kids

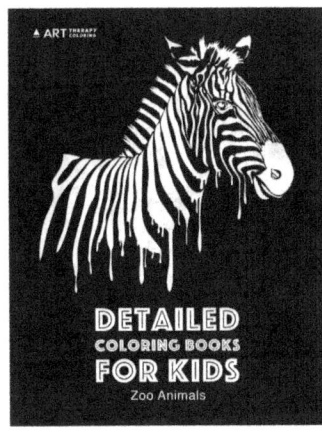

DETAILED COLORING BOOKS **FOR KIDS**
Zoo Animals

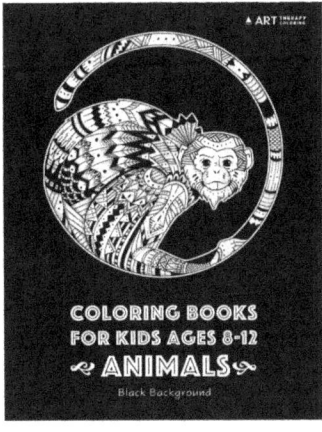

COLORING BOOKS FOR KIDS AGES 8-12 ~ANIMALS~
Black Background

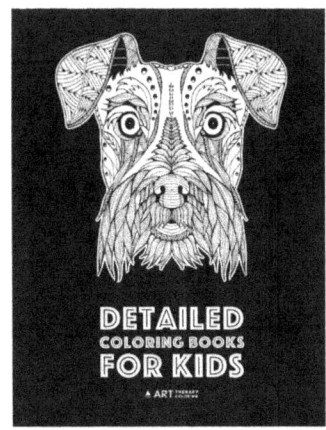

DETAILED COLORING BOOKS **FOR KIDS**

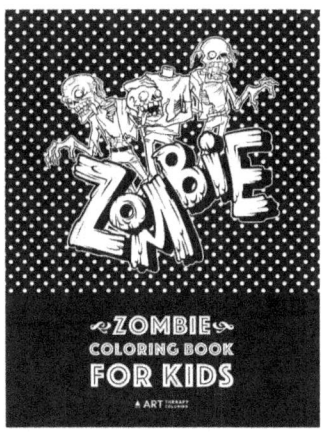

~ZOMBIE~ COLORING BOOK **FOR KIDS**

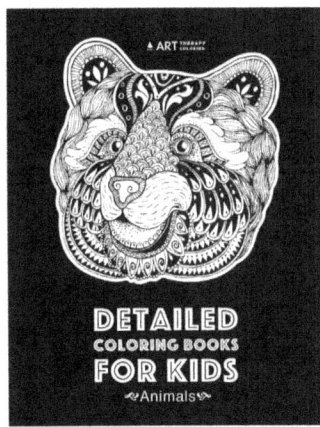

DETAILED COLORING BOOKS **FOR KIDS** ~Animals~

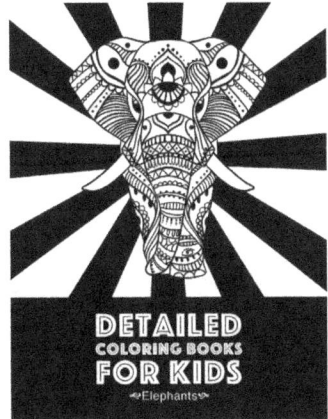

DETAILED COLORING BOOKS **FOR KIDS** ~Elephants~

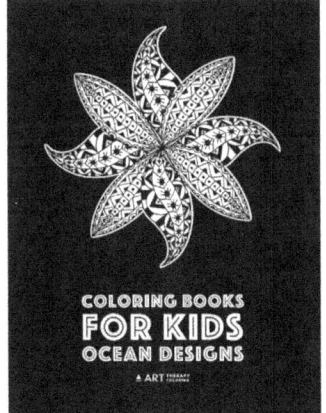

COLORING BOOKS **FOR KIDS** OCEAN DESIGNS

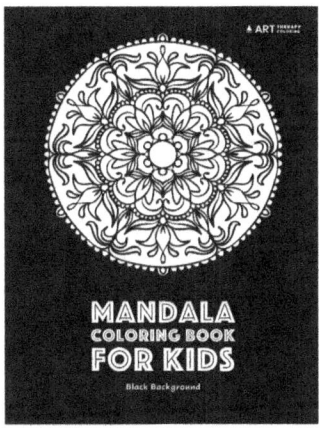

MANDALA COLORING BOOK **FOR KIDS**
Black Background

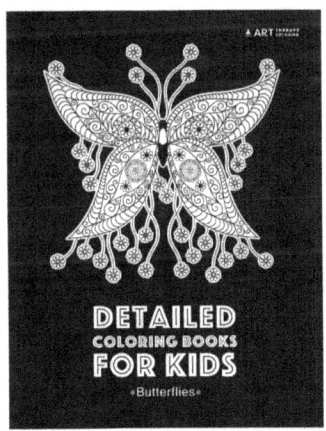

DETAILED COLORING BOOKS **FOR KIDS** ~Butterflies~

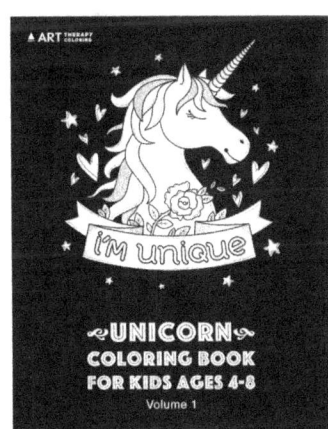

~UNICORN~ COLORING BOOK FOR KIDS AGES 4-8
Volume 1

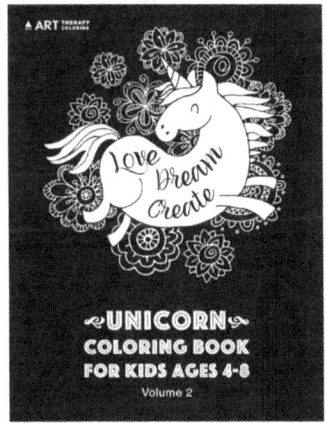

~UNICORN~ COLORING BOOK FOR KIDS AGES 4-8
Volume 2

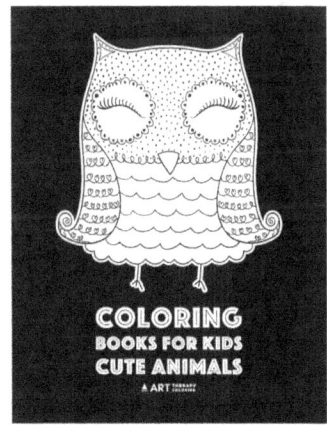

COLORING BOOKS FOR KIDS CUTE ANIMALS

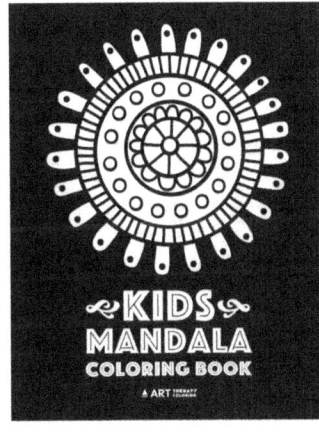

~KIDS~ MANDALA COLORING BOOK

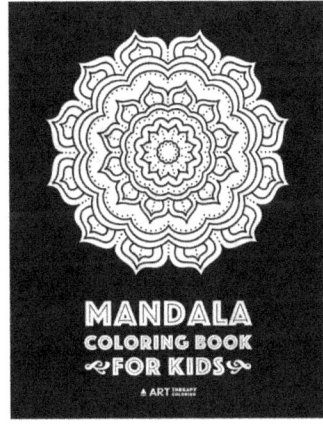

MANDALA COLORING BOOK ~FOR KIDS~

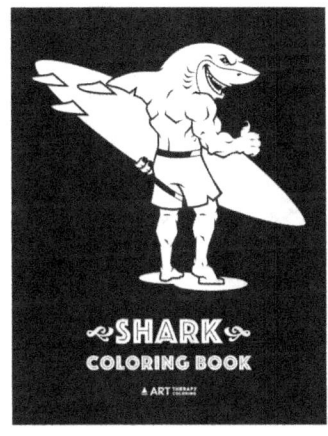

~SHARK~ COLORING BOOK

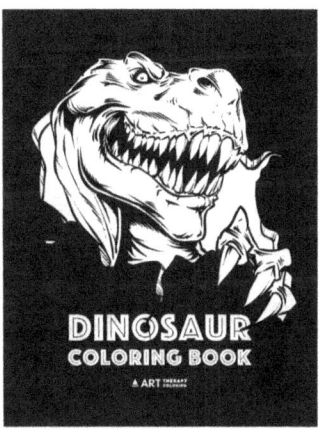

DINOSAUR COLORING BOOK

Coloring Books For Girls

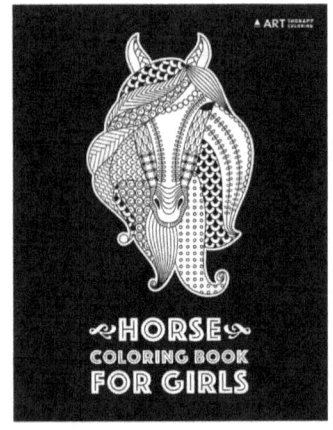

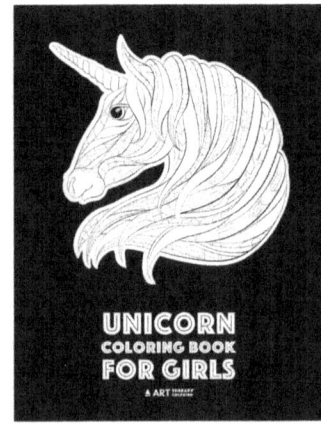

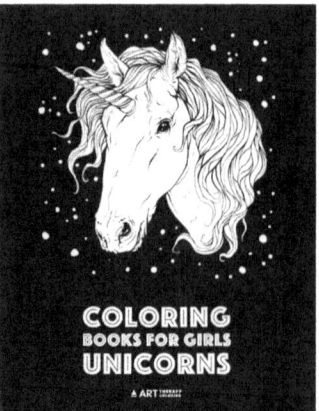

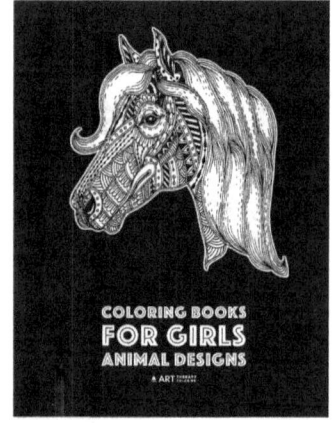

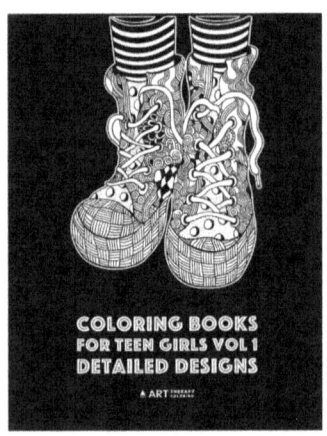

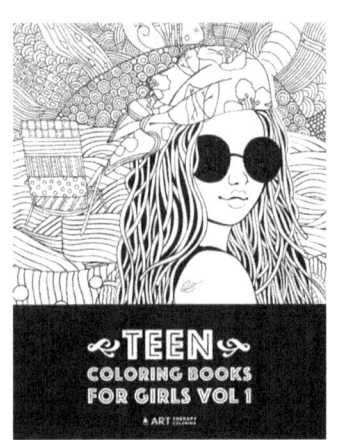

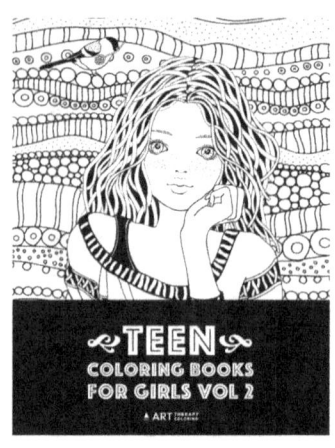

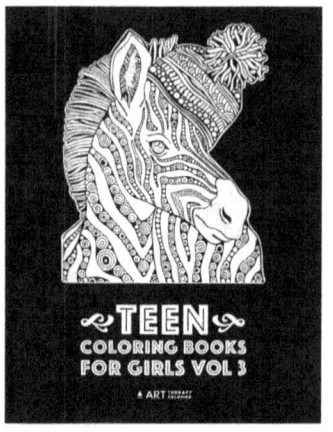

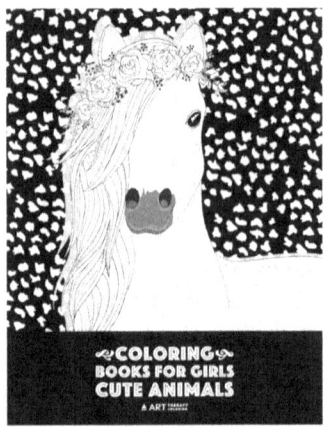

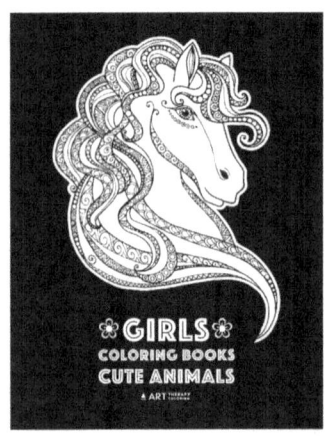

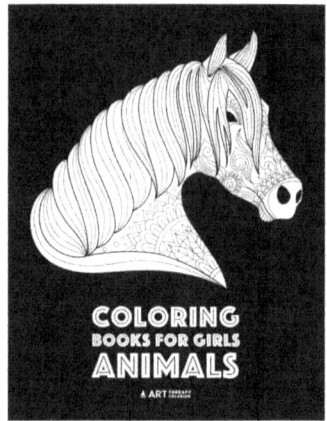

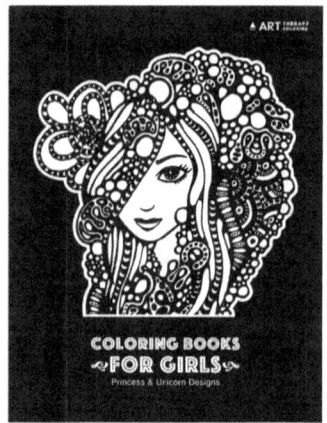

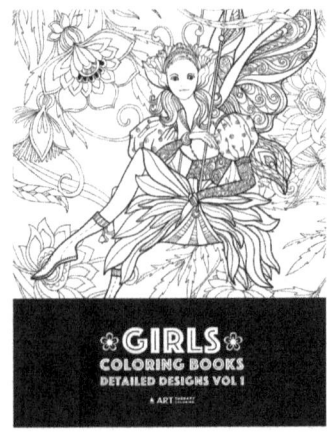

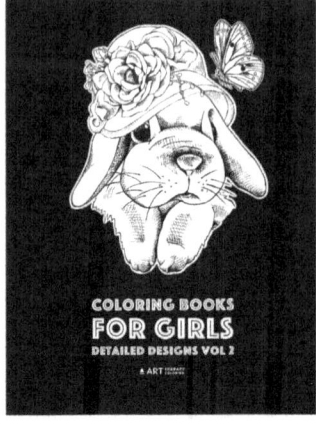

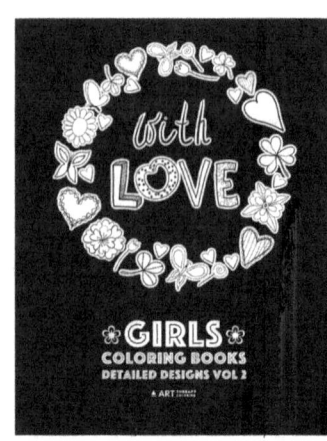

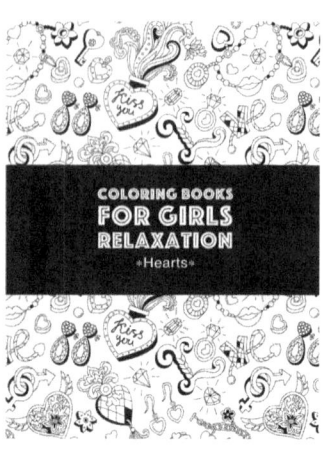

Coloring Books For Boys

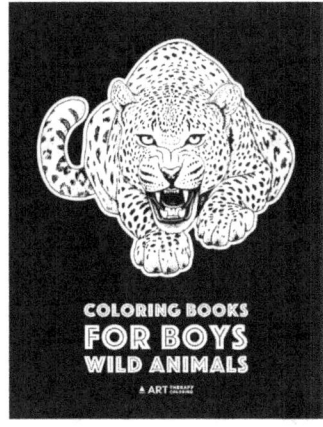

COLORING BOOKS
FOR BOYS
WILD ANIMALS

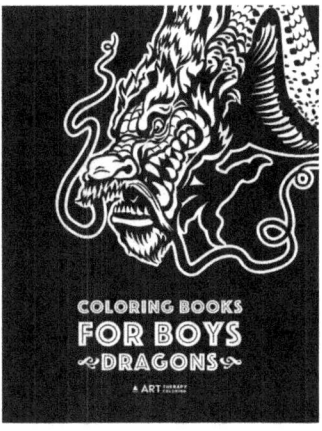

COLORING BOOKS
FOR BOYS
DRAGONS

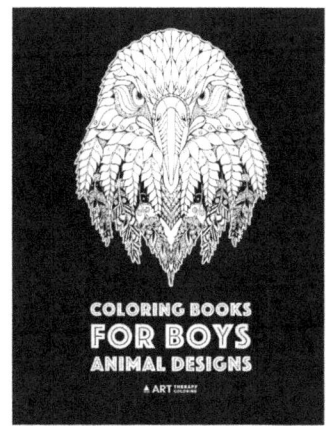

COLORING BOOKS
FOR BOYS
ANIMAL DESIGNS

COLORING BOOKS
FOR BOYS
OCEAN DESIGNS
Black Background

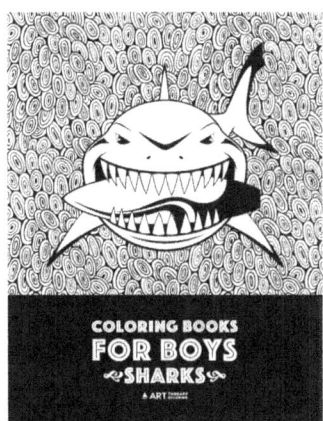

COLORING BOOKS
FOR BOYS
SHARKS

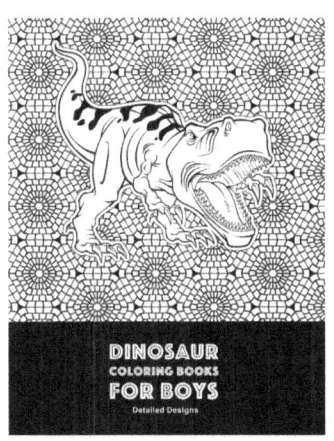

DINOSAUR
COLORING BOOKS
FOR BOYS
Detailed Designs

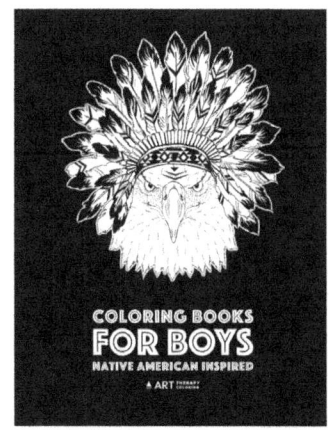

COLORING BOOKS
FOR BOYS
NATIVE AMERICAN INSPIRED

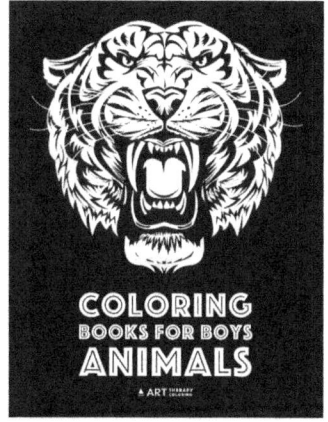

COLORING
BOOKS FOR BOYS
ANIMALS

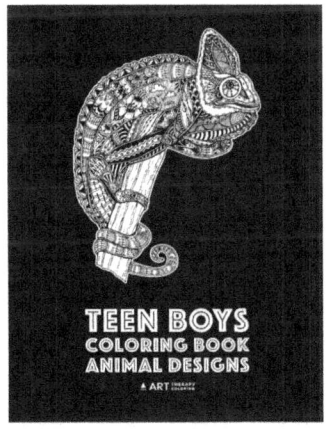

TEEN BOYS
COLORING BOOK
ANIMAL DESIGNS

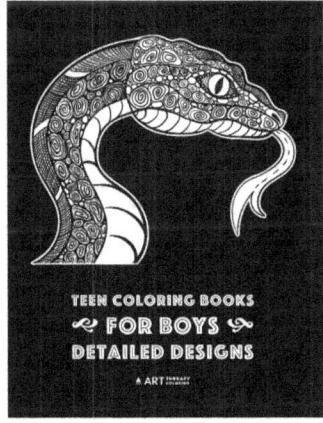

TEEN COLORING BOOKS
FOR BOYS
DETAILED DESIGNS

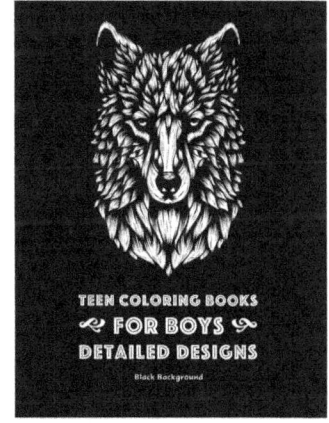

TEEN COLORING BOOKS
FOR BOYS
DETAILED DESIGNS
Black Background

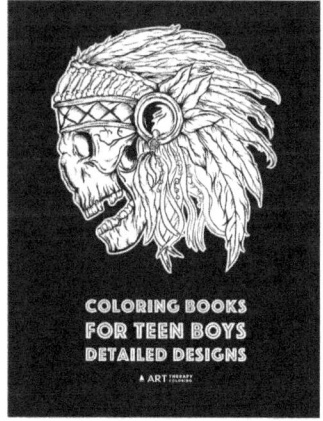

COLORING BOOKS
FOR TEEN BOYS
DETAILED DESIGNS

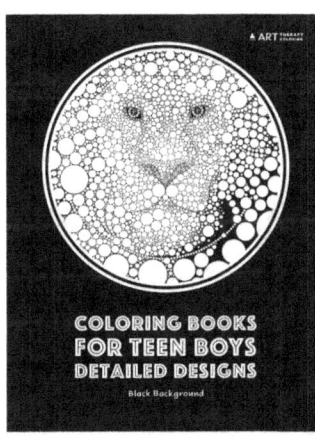

COLORING BOOKS
FOR TEEN BOYS
DETAILED DESIGNS
Black Background

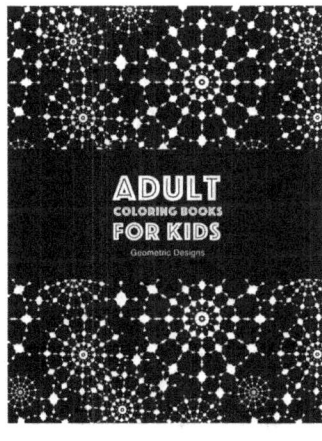

ADULT
COLORING BOOKS
FOR KIDS
Geometric Designs

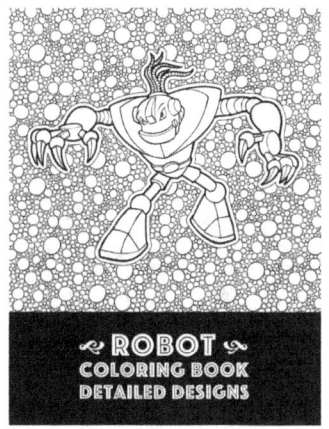

ROBOT
COLORING BOOK
DETAILED DESIGNS

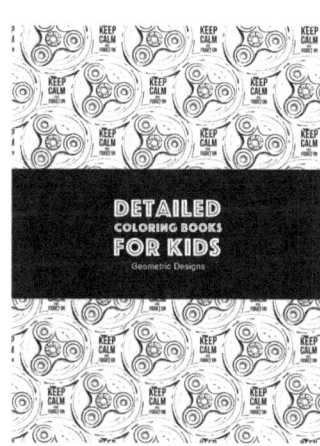

DETAILED
COLORING BOOKS
FOR KIDS
Geometric Designs

Art Therapy Coloring Books

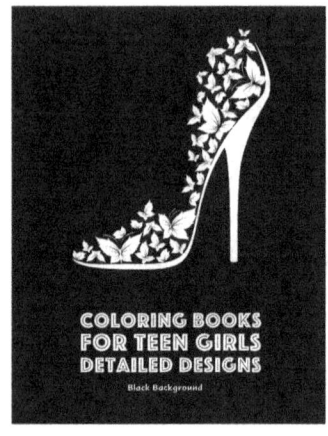

COLORING BOOKS
FOR TEEN GIRLS
DETAILED DESIGNS
Black Background

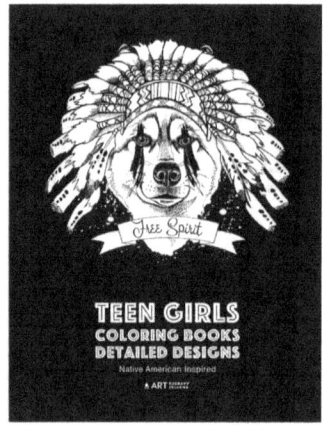

TEEN GIRLS
COLORING BOOKS
DETAILED DESIGNS
Native American Inspired

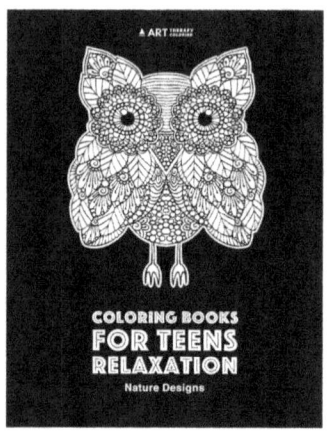

COLORING BOOKS
FOR TEENS
RELAXATION
Nature Designs

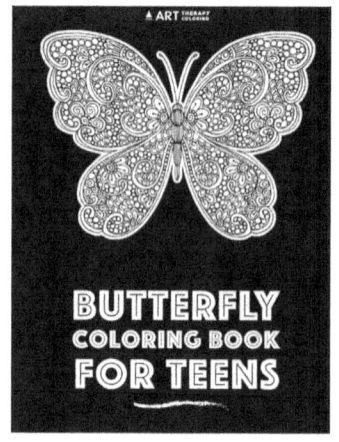

BUTTERFLY
COLORING BOOK
FOR TEENS

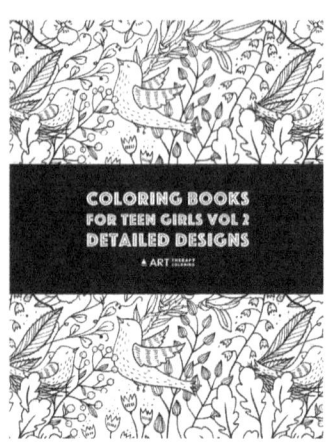

COLORING BOOKS
FOR TEEN GIRLS VOL 2
DETAILED DESIGNS

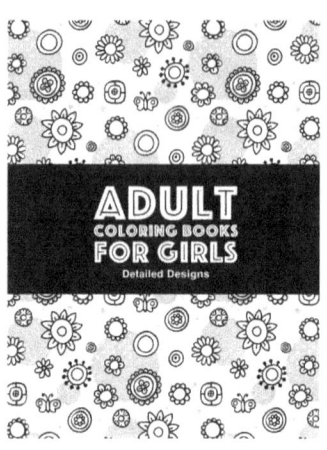

ADULT
COLORING BOOKS
FOR GIRLS
Detailed Designs

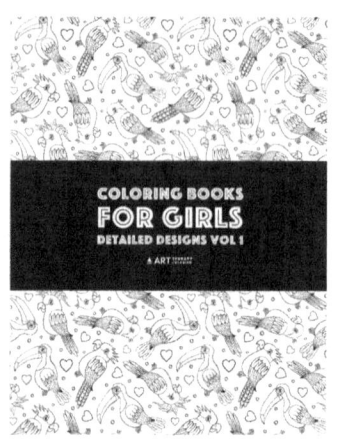

COLORING BOOKS
FOR GIRLS
DETAILED DESIGNS VOL 1

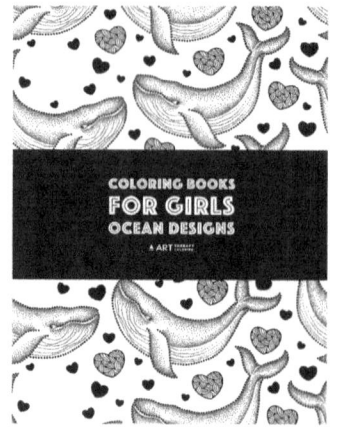

COLORING BOOKS
FOR GIRLS
OCEAN DESIGNS

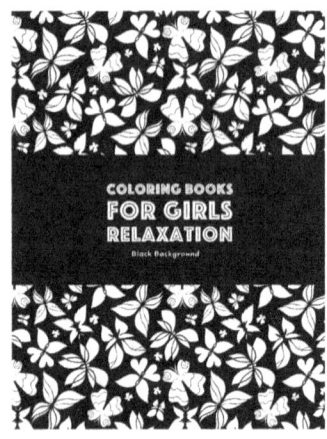

COLORING BOOKS
FOR GIRLS
RELAXATION
Black Background

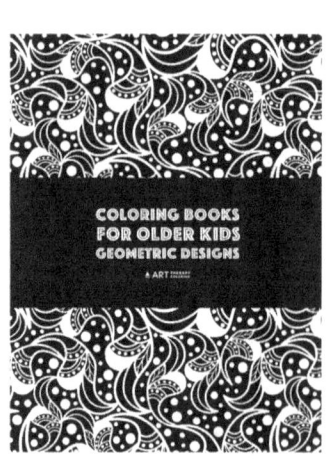

COLORING BOOKS
FOR OLDER KIDS
GEOMETRIC DESIGNS

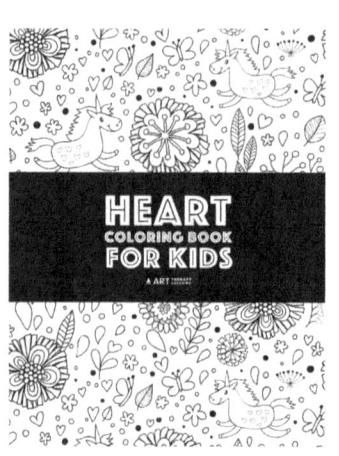

HEART
COLORING BOOK
FOR KIDS

DETAILED
COLORING BOOKS
FOR KIDS
Ocean Designs

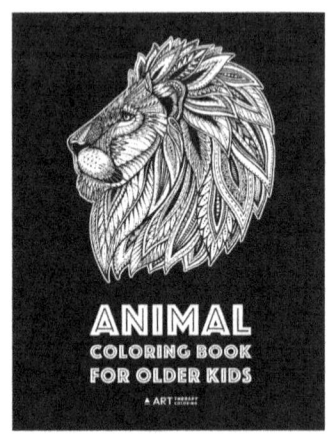

ANIMAL
COLORING BOOK
FOR OLDER KIDS

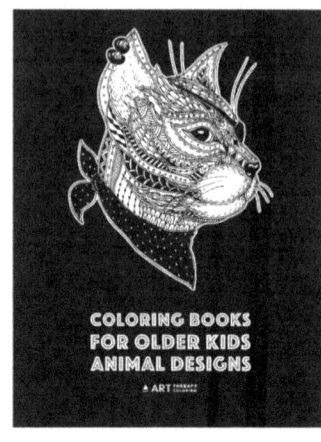

COLORING BOOKS
FOR OLDER KIDS
ANIMAL DESIGNS

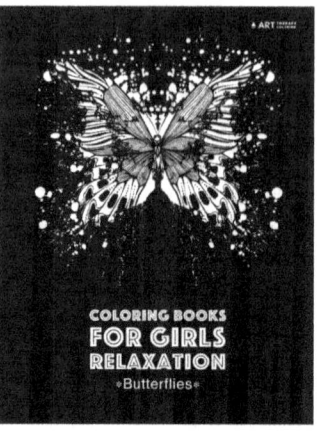

COLORING BOOKS
FOR GIRLS
RELAXATION
Butterflies

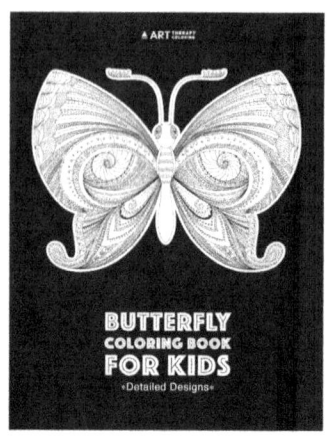

BUTTERFLY
COLORING BOOK
FOR KIDS
Detailed Designs

Coloring Books For Teens

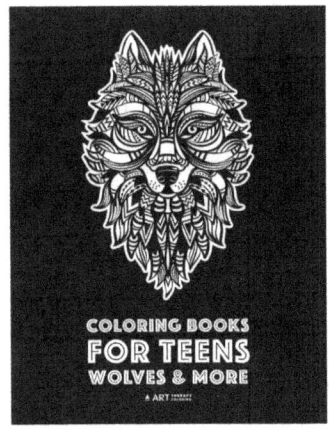

**COLORING BOOKS
FOR TEENS
WOLVES & MORE**

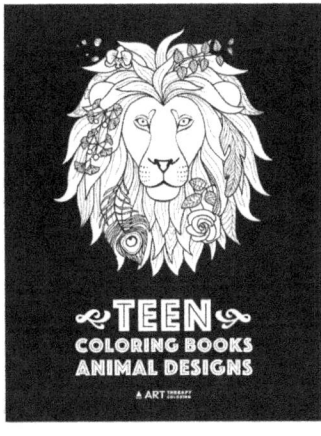

**TEEN
COLORING BOOKS
ANIMAL DESIGNS**

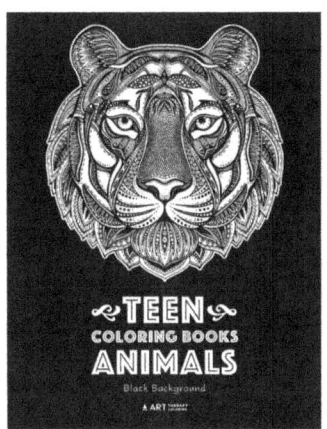

**TEEN
COLORING BOOKS
ANIMALS**
Black Background

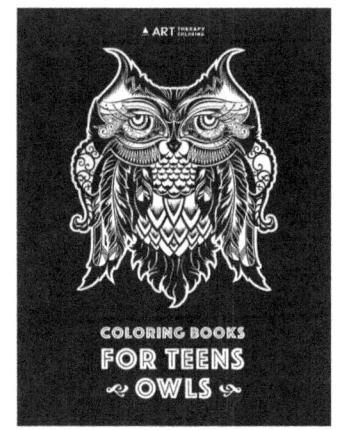

**COLORING BOOKS
FOR TEENS
OWLS**

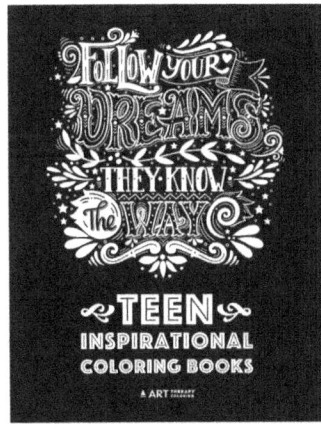

**TEEN
INSPIRATIONAL
COLORING BOOKS**

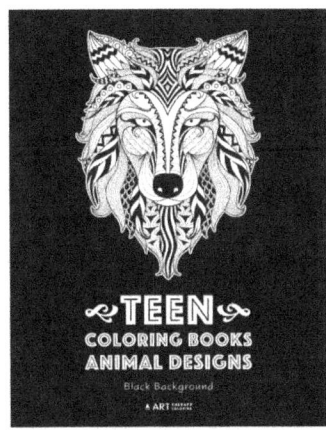

**TEEN
COLORING BOOKS
ANIMAL DESIGNS**
Black Background

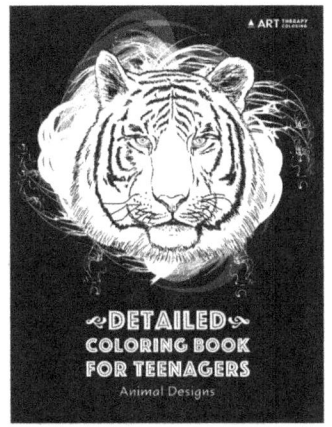

**DETAILED
COLORING BOOK
FOR TEENAGERS**
Animal Designs

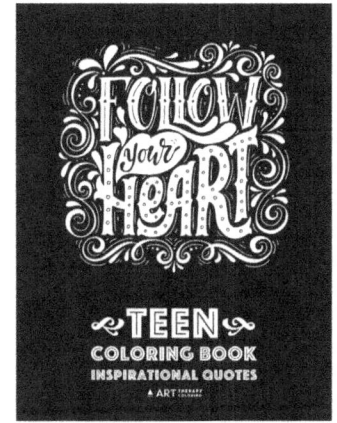

**TEEN
COLORING BOOK
INSPIRATIONAL QUOTES**

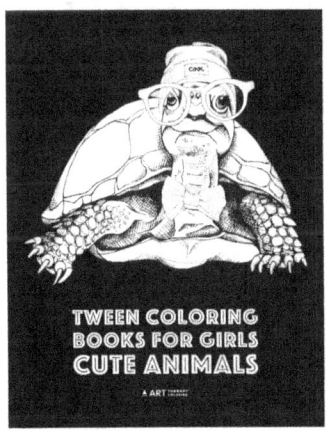

**TWEEN COLORING
BOOKS FOR GIRLS
CUTE ANIMALS**

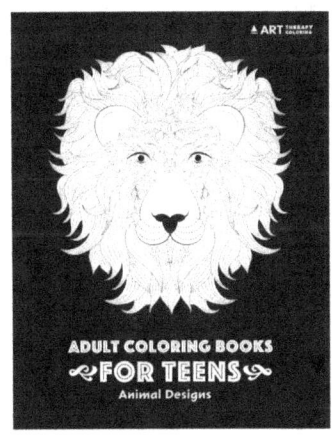

**ADULT COLORING BOOKS
FOR TEENS**
Animal Designs

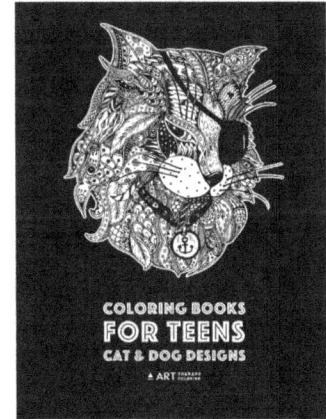

**COLORING BOOKS
FOR TEENS
CAT & DOG DESIGNS**

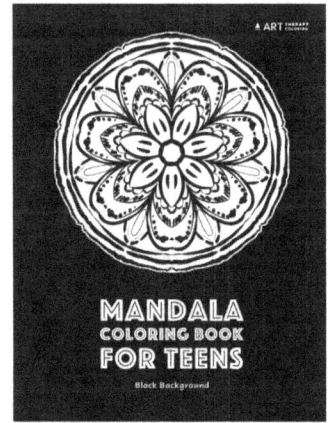

**MANDALA
COLORING BOOK
FOR TEENS**
Black Background

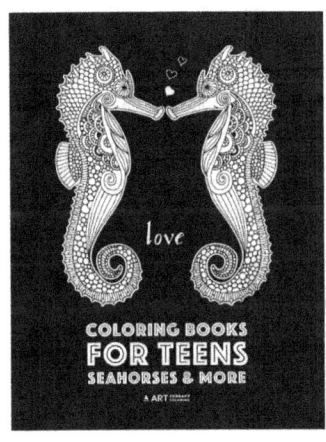

**COLORING BOOKS
FOR TEENS
SEAHORSES & MORE**

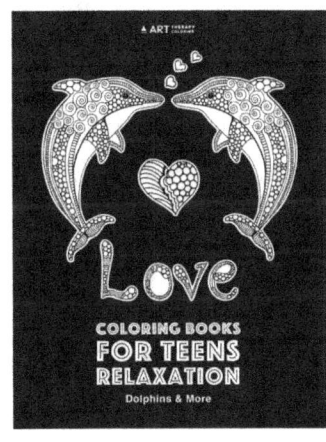

**COLORING BOOKS
FOR TEENS
RELAXATION**
Dolphins & More

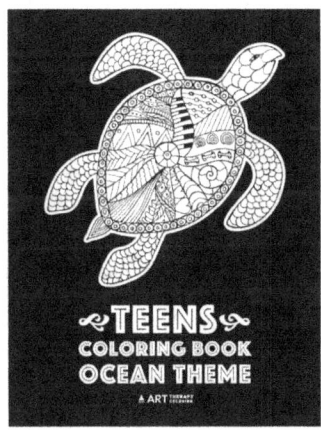

**TEENS
COLORING BOOK
OCEAN THEME**

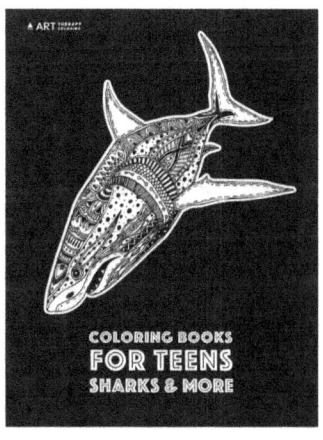

**COLORING BOOKS
FOR TEENS
SHARKS & MORE**

Coloring Books For Teens

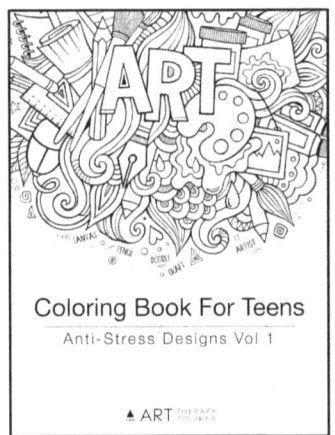

Coloring Book For Teens

Anti-Stress Designs Vol 1

ART THERAPY COLORING

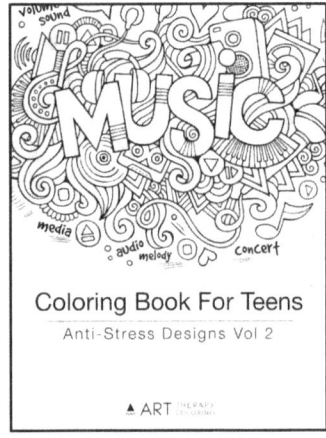

Coloring Book For Teens

Anti-Stress Designs Vol 2

ART THERAPY COLORING

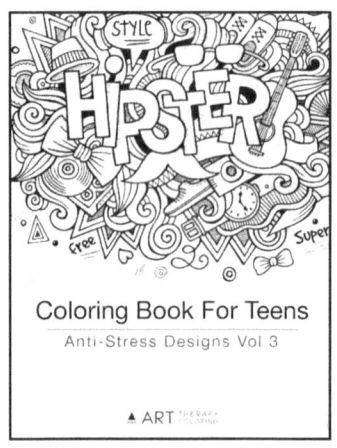

Coloring Book For Teens

Anti-Stress Designs Vol 3

ART THERAPY COLORING

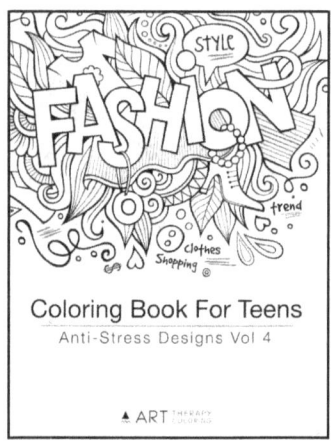

Coloring Book For Teens

Anti-Stress Designs Vol 4

ART THERAPY COLORING

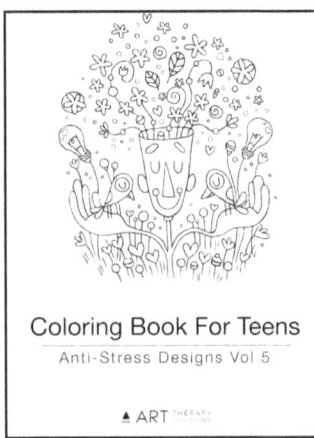

Coloring Book For Teens

Anti-Stress Designs Vol 5

ART THERAPY COLORING

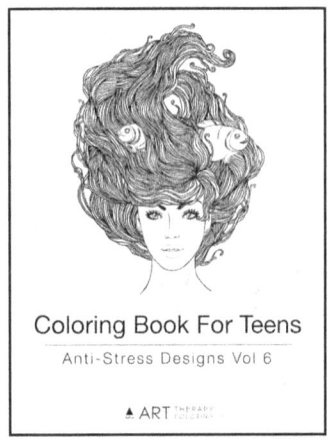

Coloring Book For Teens

Anti-Stress Designs Vol 6

ART THERAPY COLORING

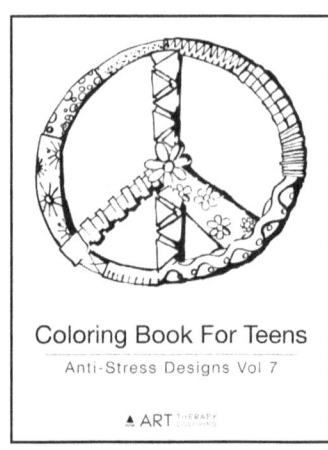

Coloring Book For Teens

Anti-Stress Designs Vol 7

ART THERAPY COLORING

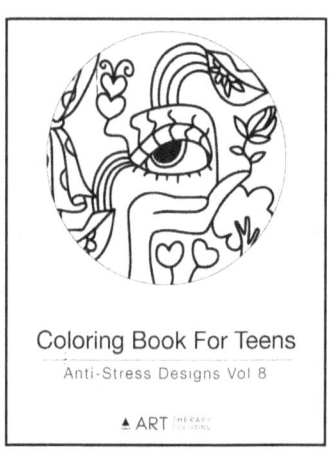

Coloring Book For Teens

Anti-Stress Designs Vol 8

ART THERAPY COLORING

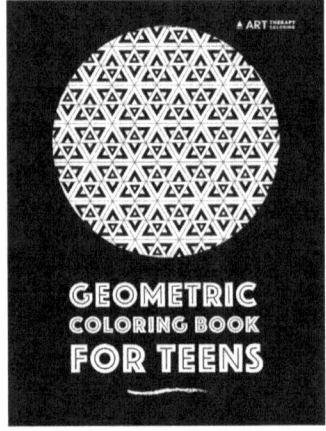

GEOMETRIC COLORING BOOK FOR TEENS

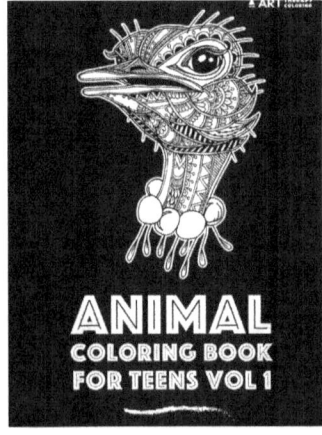

ANIMAL COLORING BOOK FOR TEENS VOL 1

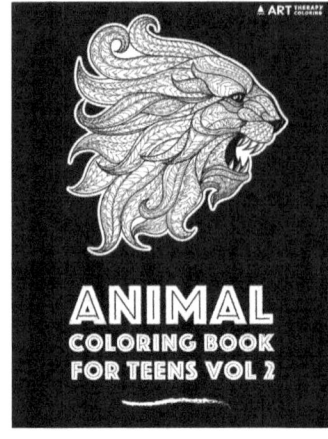

ANIMAL COLORING BOOK FOR TEENS VOL 2

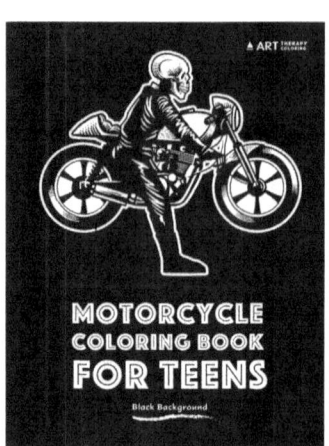

MOTORCYCLE COLORING BOOK FOR TEENS

Black Background

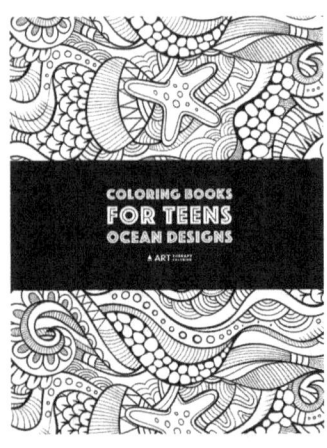

COLORING BOOKS FOR TEENS OCEAN DESIGNS

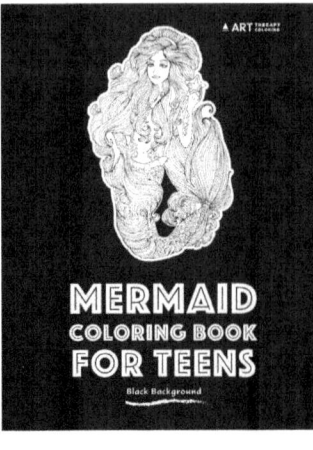

MERMAID COLORING BOOK FOR TEENS

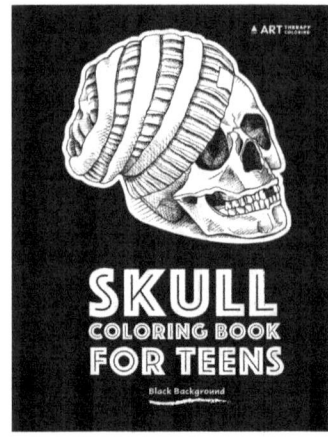

SKULL COLORING BOOK FOR TEENS

Black Background

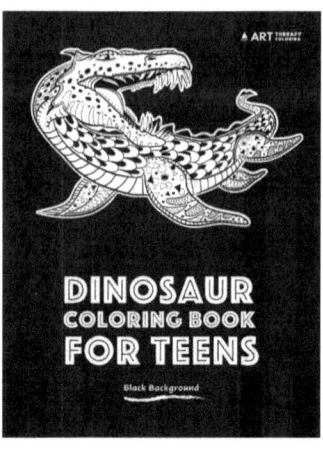

DINOSAUR COLORING BOOK FOR TEENS

Black Background

Coloring Books For Adults

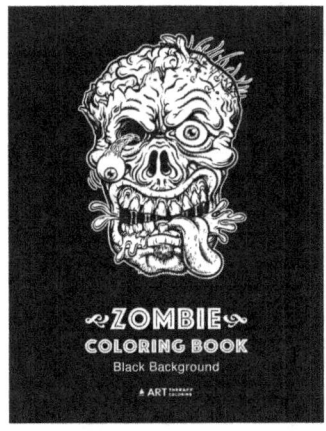

ZOMBIE
COLORING BOOK
Black Background

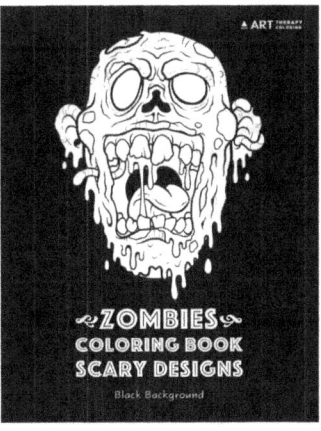

ZOMBIES
COLORING BOOK
SCARY DESIGNS
Black Background

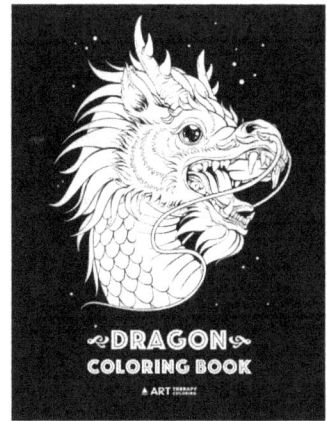

DRAGON
COLORING BOOK

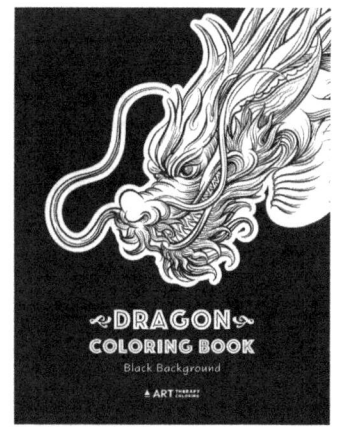

DRAGON
COLORING BOOK
Black Background

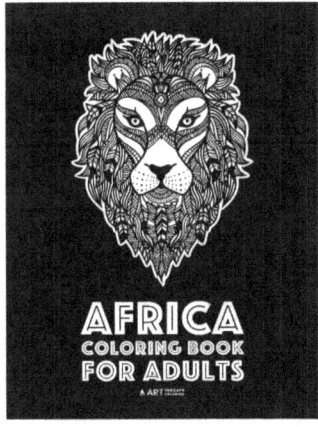

AFRICA
COLORING BOOK
FOR ADULTS

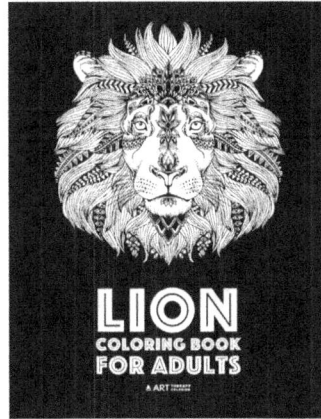

LION
COLORING BOOK
FOR ADULTS

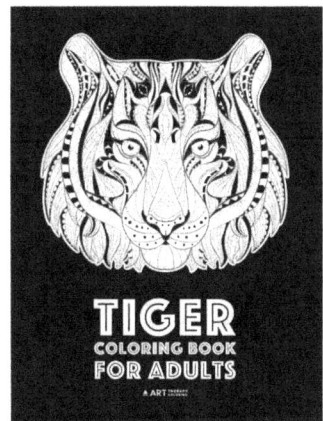

TIGER
COLORING BOOK
FOR ADULTS

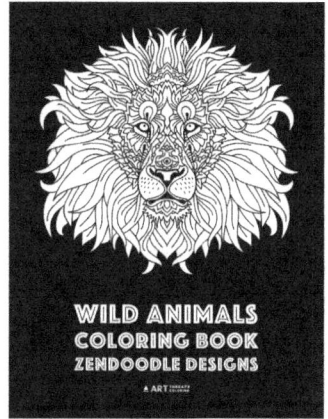

WILD ANIMALS
COLORING BOOK
ZENDOODLE DESIGNS

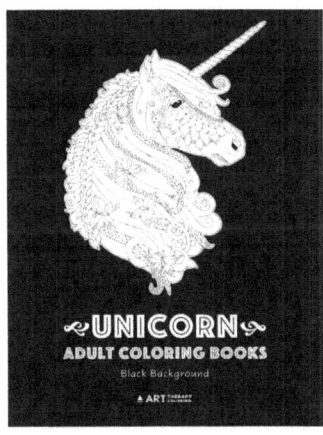

UNICORN
ADULT COLORING BOOKS
Black Background

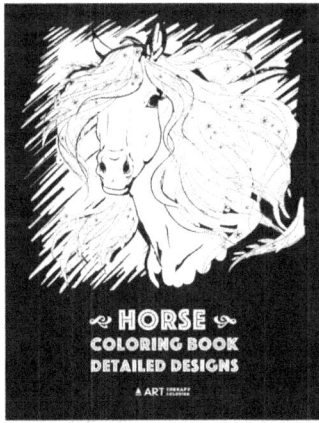

HORSE
COLORING BOOK
DETAILED DESIGNS

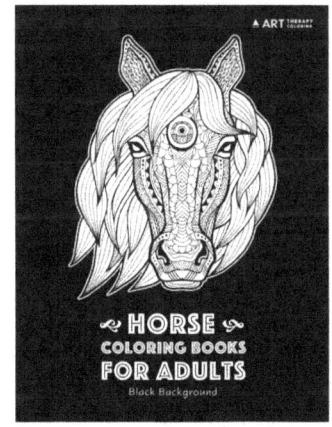

HORSE
COLORING BOOKS
FOR ADULTS
Black Background

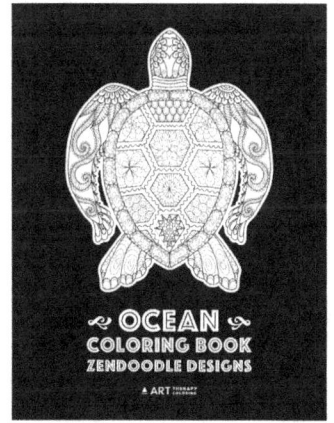

OCEAN
COLORING BOOK
ZENDOODLE DESIGNS

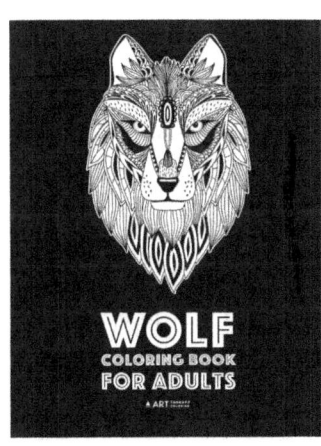

WOLF
COLORING BOOK
FOR ADULTS

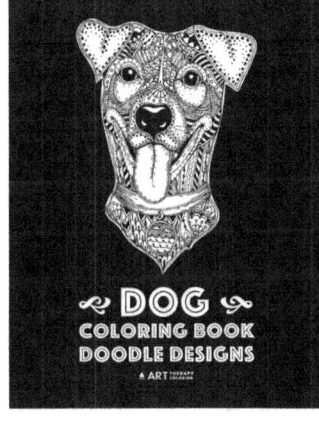

DOG
COLORING BOOK
DOODLE DESIGNS

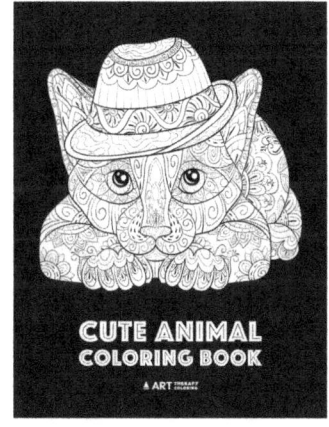

CUTE ANIMAL
COLORING BOOK

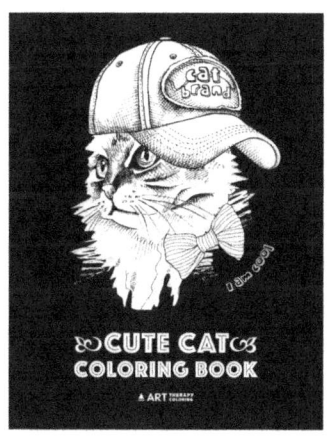

CUTE CAT
COLORING BOOK

Coloring Books For Adults

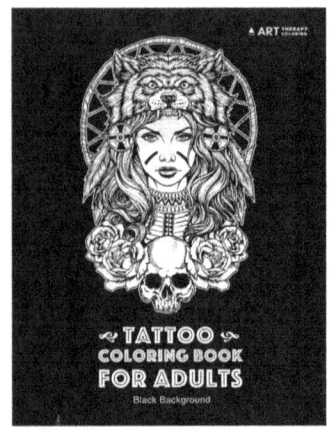

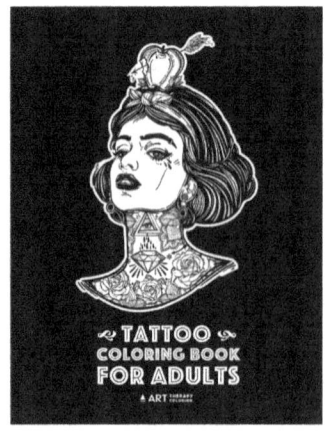

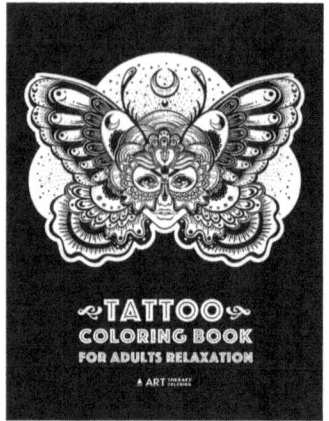

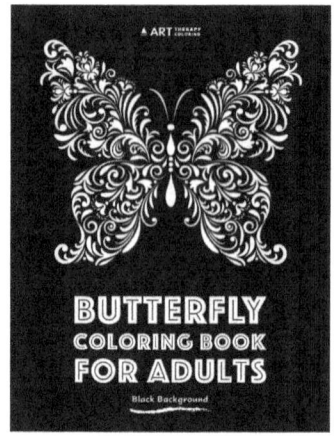

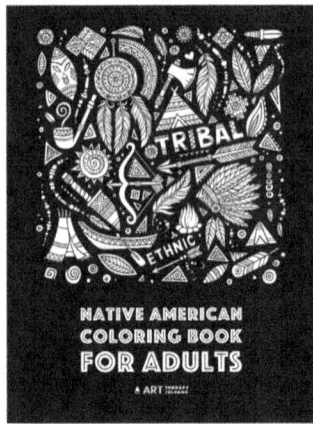

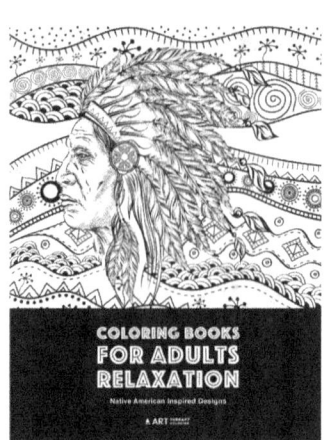

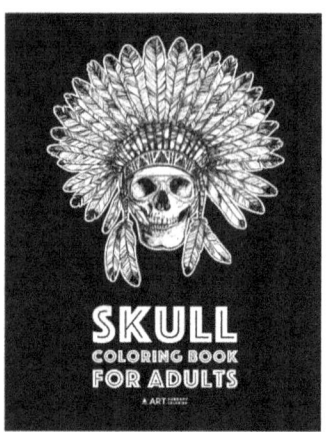

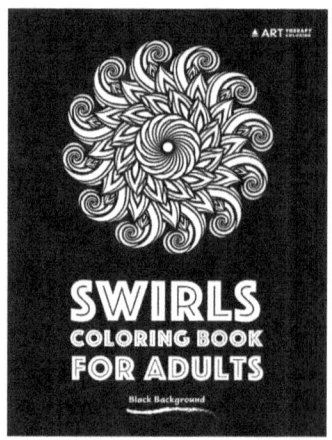

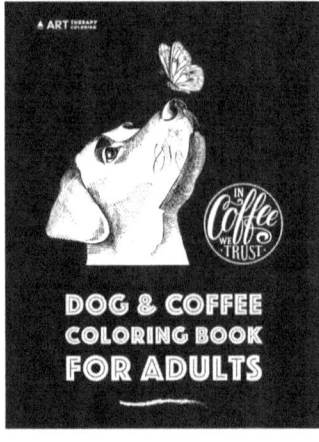

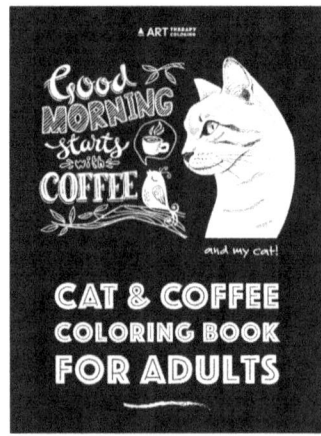

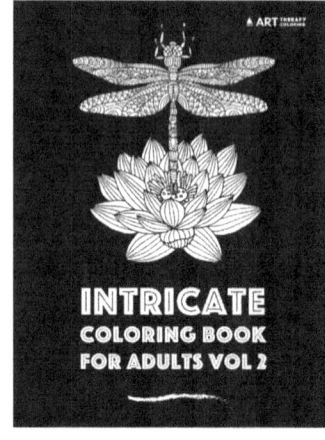

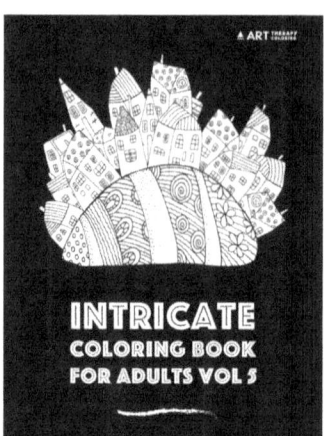

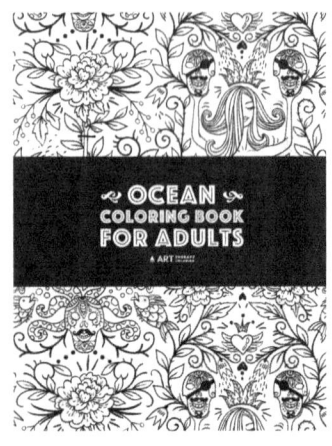

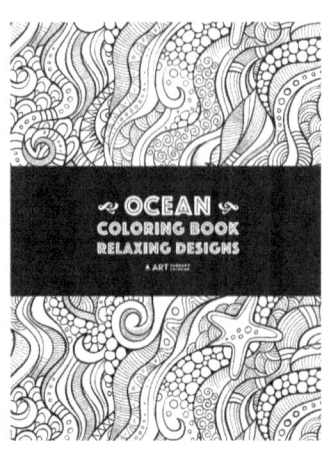

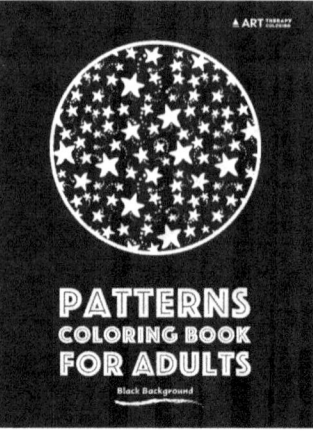

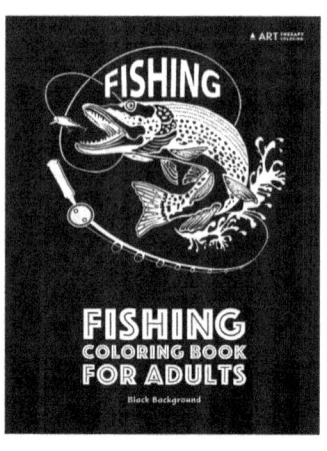

Coloring Books For Adults

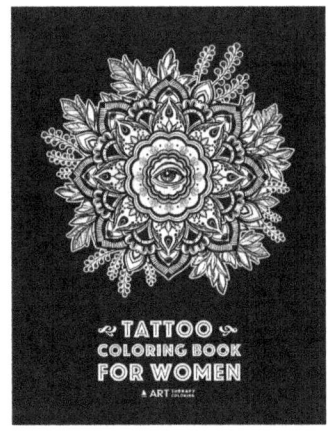

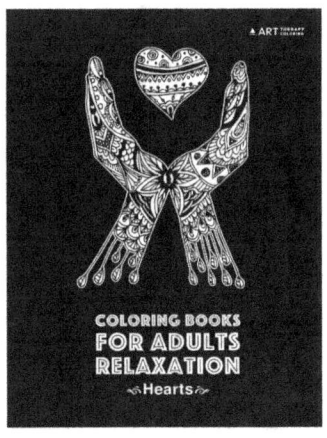

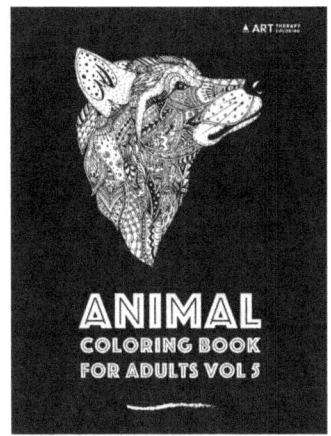

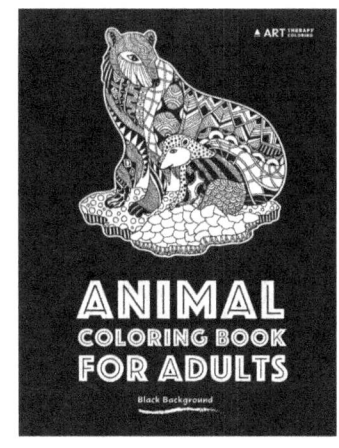

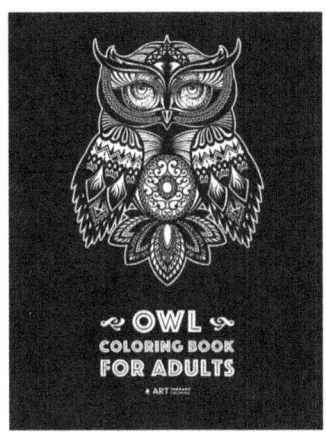

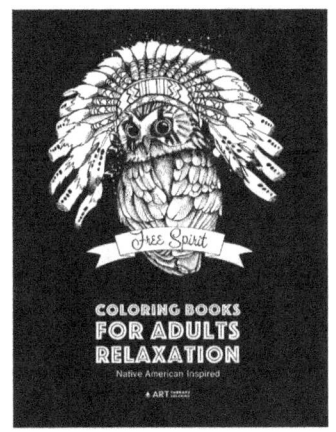

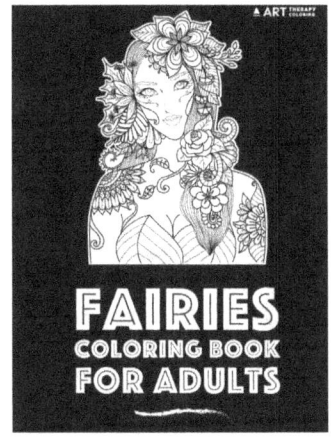

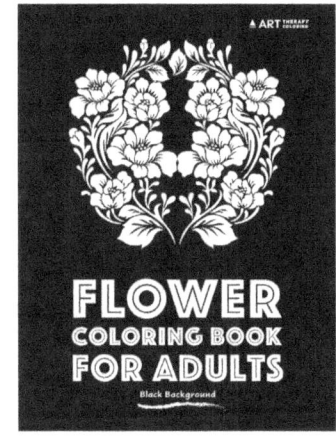

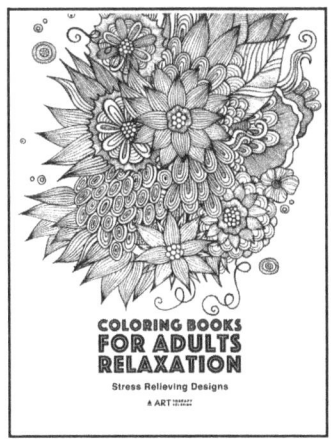

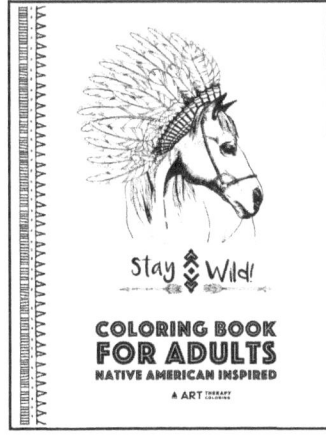

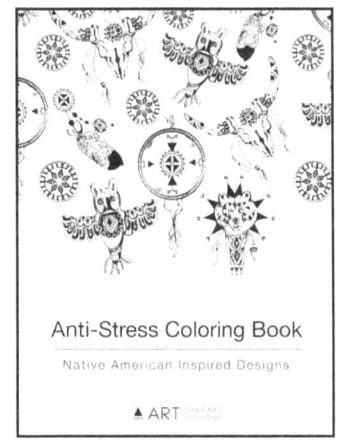

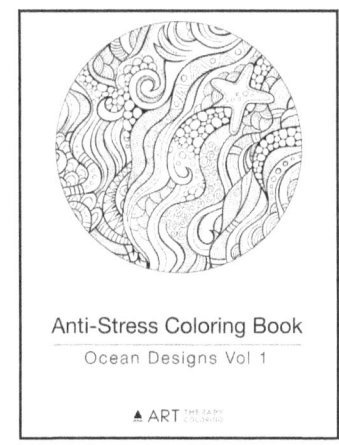

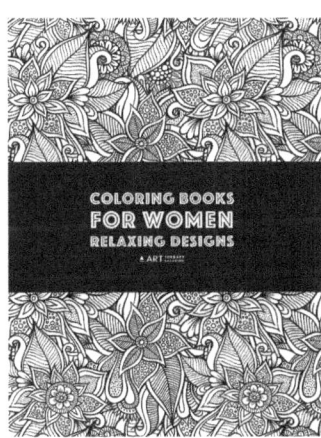

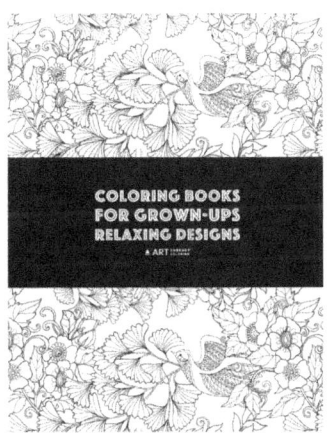

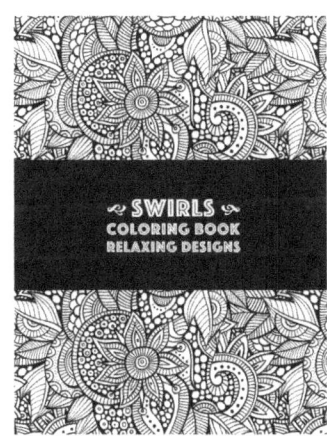

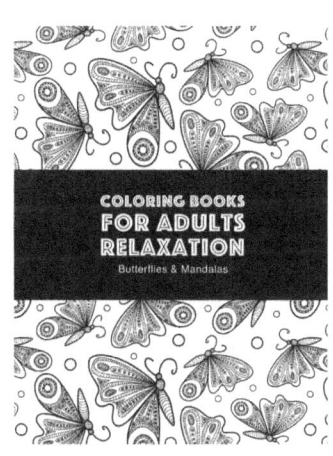

Coloring Books For Seniors

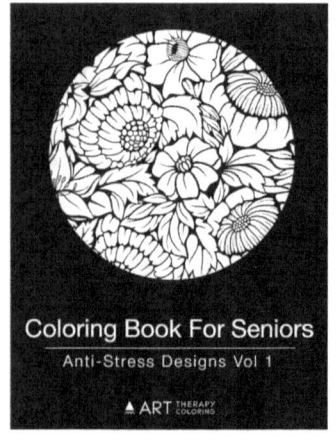

Coloring Book For Seniors
Anti-Stress Designs Vol 1
ART THERAPY COLORING

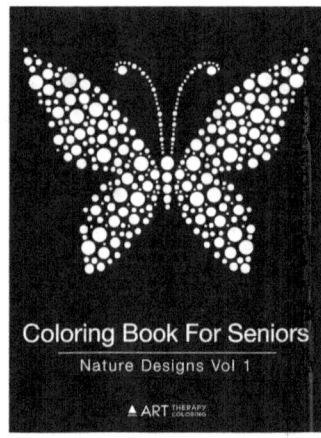

Coloring Book For Seniors
Nature Designs Vol 1
ART THERAPY COLORING

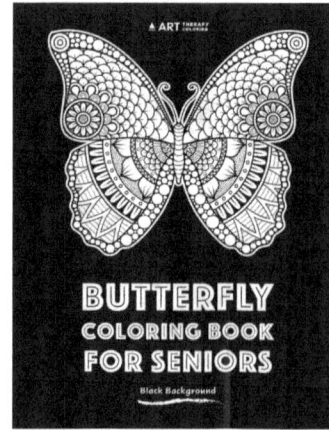

BUTTERFLY
COLORING BOOK
FOR SENIORS
Black Background

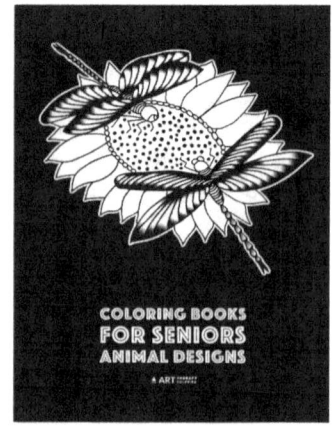

COLORING BOOKS
FOR SENIORS
ANIMAL DESIGNS
ART THERAPY COLORING

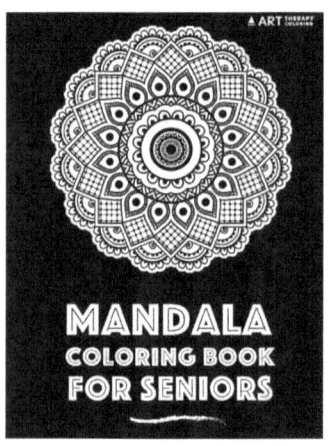

MANDALA
COLORING BOOK
FOR SENIORS

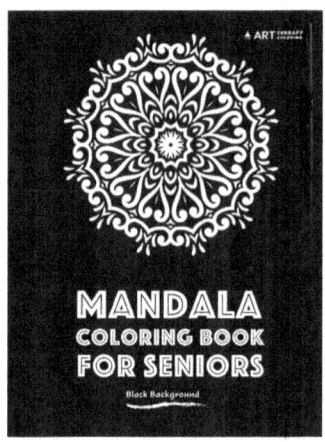

MANDALA
COLORING BOOK
FOR SENIORS
Black Background

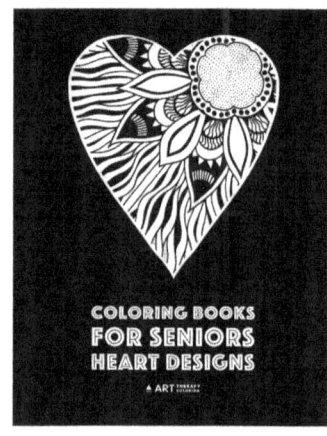

COLORING BOOKS
FOR SENIORS
HEART DESIGNS
ART THERAPY COLORING

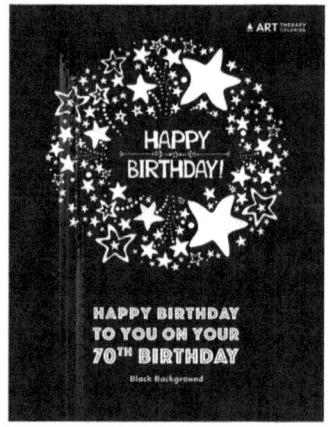

HAPPY BIRTHDAY!
HAPPY BIRTHDAY
TO YOU ON YOUR
70TH BIRTHDAY
Black Background

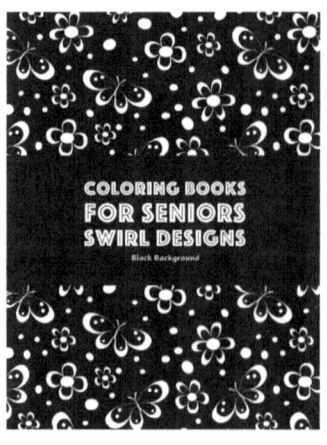

COLORING BOOKS
FOR SENIORS
SWIRL DESIGNS
Black Background

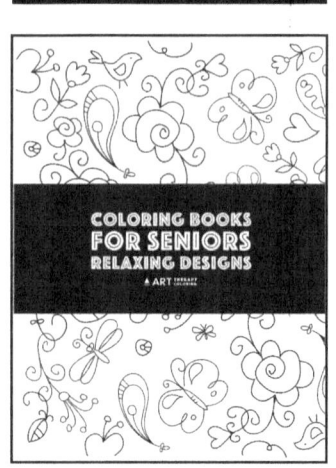

COLORING BOOKS
FOR SENIORS
RELAXING DESIGNS
ART COLORING

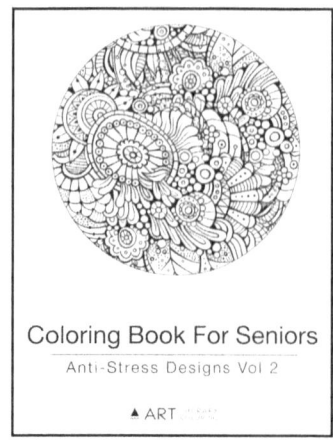

Coloring Book For Seniors
Anti-Stress Designs Vol 2
ART

Coloring Book For Seniors
Anti-Stress Designs Vol 3
ART

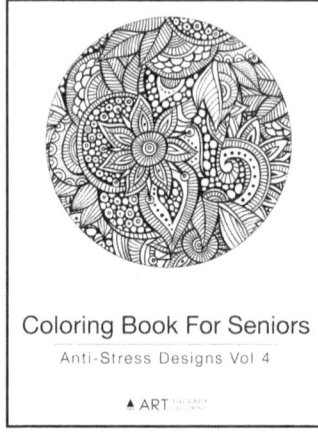

Coloring Book For Seniors
Anti-Stress Designs Vol 4
ART THERAPY COLORING

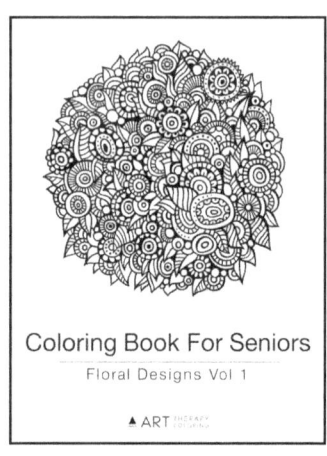

Coloring Book For Seniors
Floral Designs Vol 1
ART THERAPY COLORING

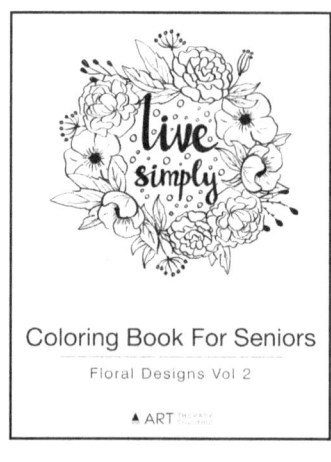

Coloring Book For Seniors
Floral Designs Vol 2
ART THERAPY COLORING

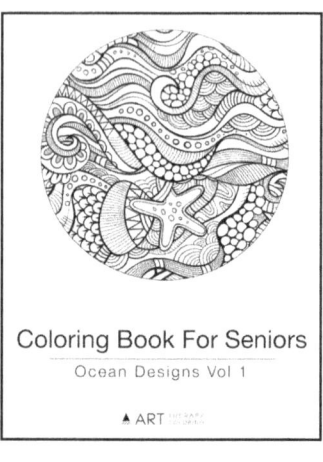

Coloring Book For Seniors
Ocean Designs Vol 1
ART THERAPY COLORING

Coloring Books For Men

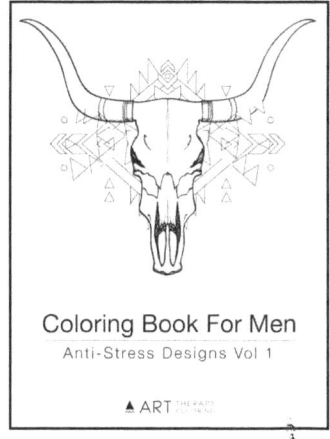

Coloring Book For Men
Anti-Stress Designs Vol 1

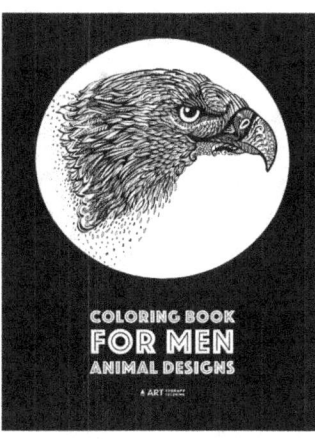

COLORING BOOK
FOR MEN
ANIMAL DESIGNS

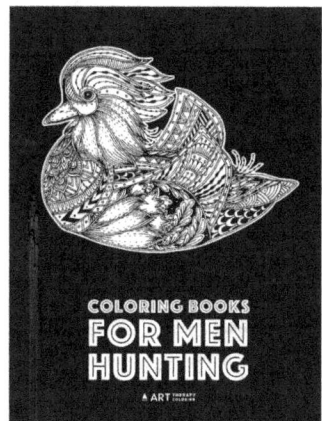

COLORING BOOKS
FOR MEN
HUNTING

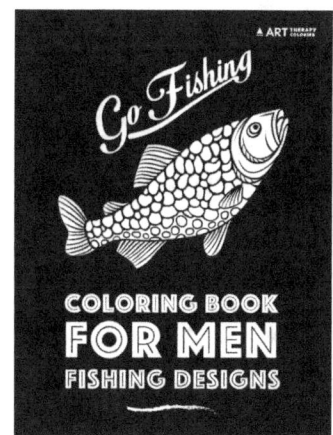

Go Fishing
COLORING BOOK
FOR MEN
FISHING DESIGNS

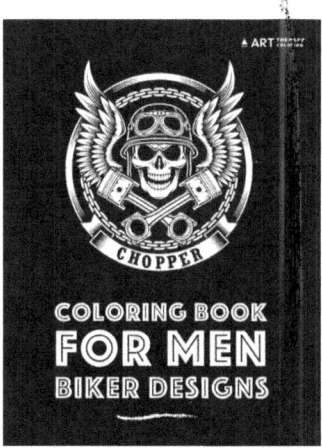

COLORING BOOK
FOR MEN
BIKER DESIGNS

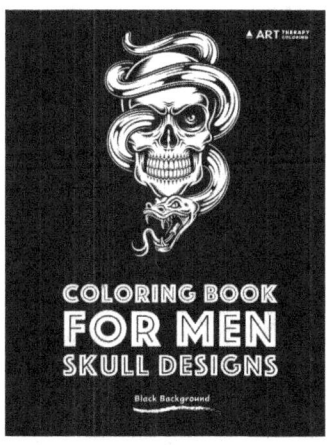

COLORING BOOK
FOR MEN
SKULL DESIGNS
Black Background

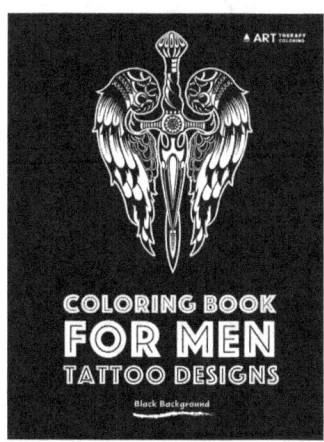

COLORING BOOK
FOR MEN
TATTOO DESIGNS
Black Background

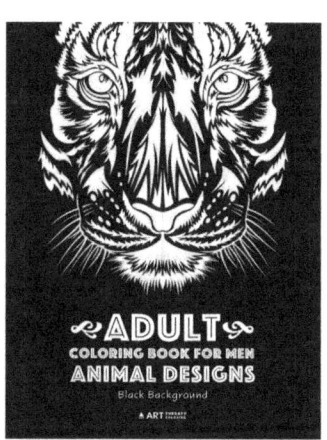

ADULT
COLORING BOOK FOR MEN
ANIMAL DESIGNS
Black Background

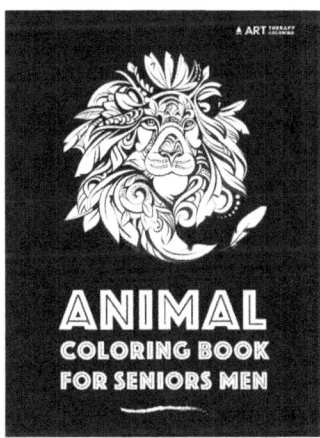

ANIMAL
COLORING BOOK
FOR SENIORS MEN

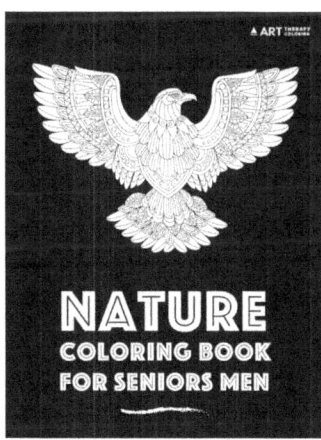

NATURE
COLORING BOOK
FOR SENIORS MEN

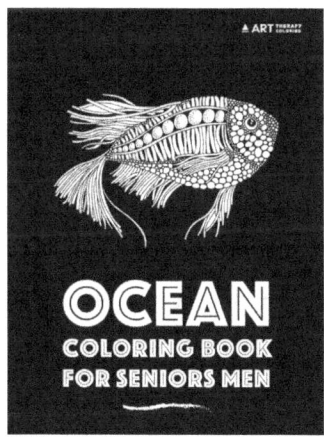

OCEAN
COLORING BOOK
FOR SENIORS MEN

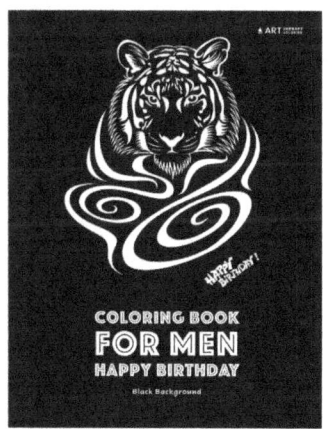

COLORING BOOK
FOR MEN
HAPPY BIRTHDAY
Black Background

Coloring Books For Special Occasions

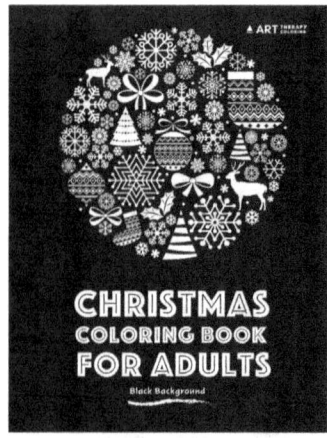

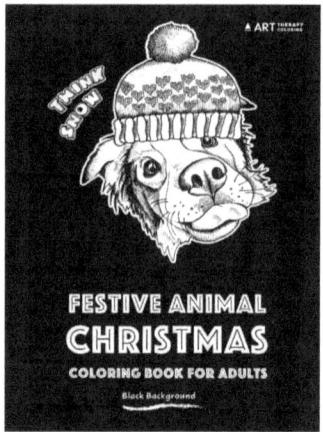

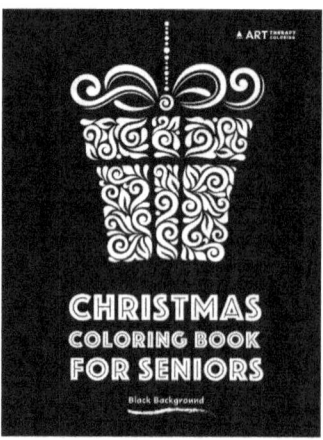

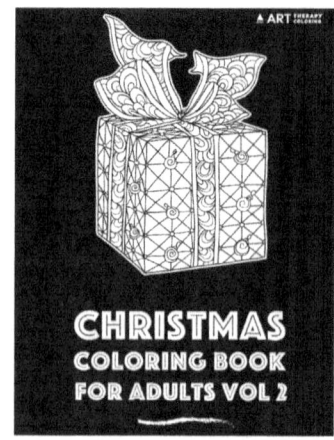

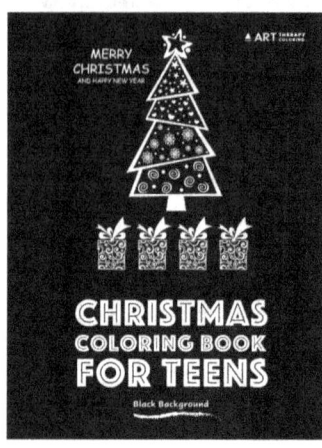

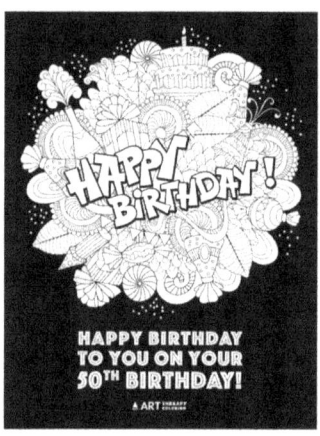

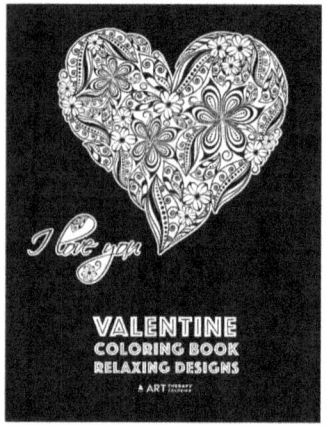

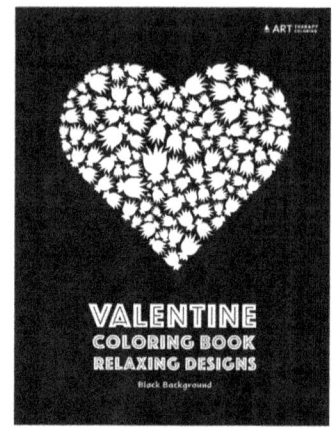

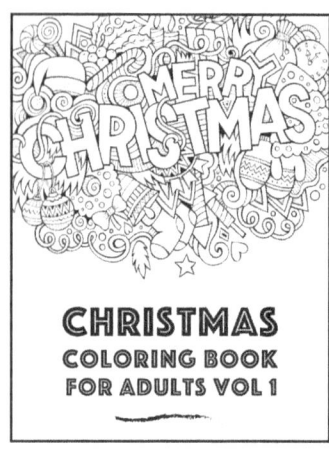

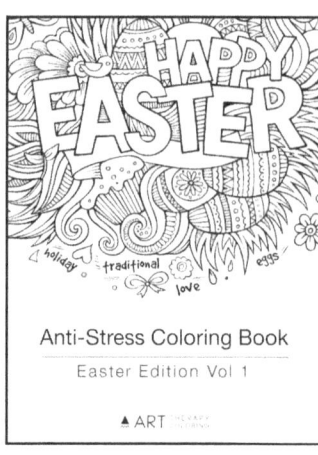

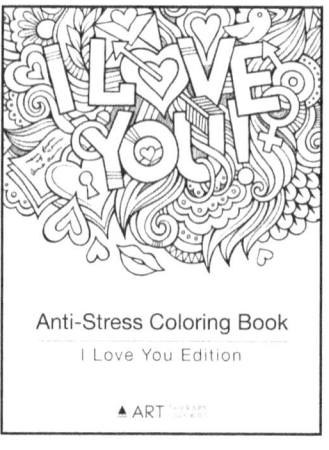

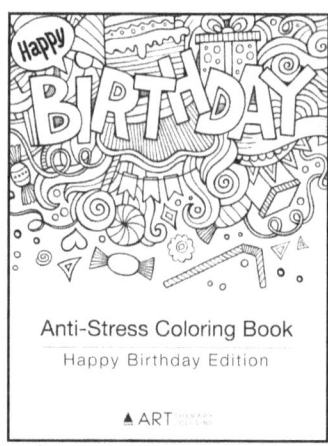

Heart Coloring Book For Kids

Published by:
Art Therapy Coloring
El Dorado Hills, California
www.arttherapycoloring.com

Shutterstock Images

ISBN: 978-1-64126-050-3

www.ingramcontent.com/pod-product-compliance
Lightning Source LLC
Chambersburg PA
CBHW081240180526
45171CB00005B/485